Butterflies and Winged Bugs Coloring and Activity Book

Coloring Pages, Mazes, Word Searches, and More!

A "Critter Activity Book"
by Julia L. Wright
from HieroGraphics Books.

Published by HieroGraphics Books as part of the "Critters Activity Book" collection created by Julia L. Wright.

If after a young person colors a page and he or she wants to remove a page for framing, please ask an adult to carefully cut it out with a very sharp knife and a ruler.

For information regarding permissions, write to:
info@hierographicsbooksllc.com

www.hierographicsbooksllc.com
Manitou Springs, CO

Cover Design by Julia L. Wright ©2020

Printed in the United States of America

First Printing, February, 2021
Second Printing, March 2026

ISBN: 978-0-9965816-8-4

This Book Belongs to

_____

_____

_____

_____

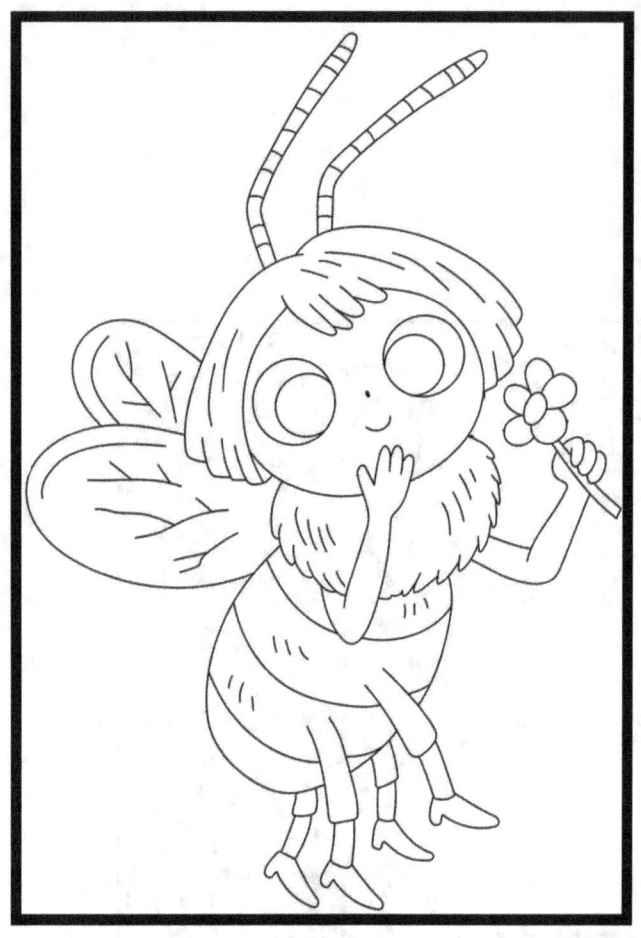

Betsy Bumble Bee would like to tell you a little about what you will find inside this coloring and activity book. She knows you must appreciate butterflies and cute bugs because you bought this book to have some fun by coloring them.

Each of the Winged Bugs have been given a name. There is a very short story about what they are doing on their page.

On many of the pages inside this book these delightful winged creatures are engaged in unusual activities for a bug. Some are delivering something to a house or painting a fence. Others are playing music or dancing to what they are hearing.

There are Mazes and two types of Word Puzzles to solve as activities to do beyond coloring these insects that can fly.

When doing the Word Search Puzzles, you will be circling the words listed above the puzzle found among a random series of letters. Some will be straight across, others will be found on an angle or spelled in a backwards manner.

One Word Search Puzzle is based on the names of the Winged Bugs in this coloring book. The second Word Search Puzzle has words that relate to the types of real bugs these fun ones are modeled on.

The Mazes have butterflies needing your help to discover the path to where there is a garden filled with flowers. There is just one path that will lead the way they must go to find flowers to help pollinate. If you find the Mazes in this activity book challenging, you might want to copy them to work on outside of the book.

The clues for the first Crossword Puzzle are questions that relate to an activity a bug is engaged in on one of the coloring pages. The next one will name a bug and have you identify the actual type of insect that it is based on. The third one will ask you to respond with the name of a bug that is doing a specific activity somewhere in this book.

There are images of butterflies floating above huge flowers with patterns on their petals to color. And round mandalas that are just big flowers or are based on images of small flowers and butterflies.

When coloring, remember these are your images to create and make them look however you like to color. Some have areas of very tiny lines, but you don't have to color in each small section. You may chose that area to be just one color, or color every other one of the tiny sections. This is meant to be a fun activity book, but maybe just a little challenging.

At the end of this book are pages where budding authors can write stories about what their favorite bugs or butterflies are doing. Aspiring artists have a space they can use to sketch an image for that story.

So it's time to start coloring butterflies, flowers and Winged Bugs or engaging in some of the activities you will find inside.

HAVE FUN!

What You Will Find On The Pages In This
Winged Bugs And Butterflies Coloring And Activity Book:

On Pages 7 to 19 you can color winged bugs engaged in many different activities.

On Pages 21 to 27 you can color butterflies and lovely flowers they are flying above.

On Pages 29 to 39 are Mazes to solve to guide a butterfly to some flowers to land upon.

On Pages 41 to 49 you will be coloring winged bugs that are either creating or enjoying music floating through the air above a grassy field.

Page 51 has a Word Search Puzzle using the names of the winged bugs.

Page 53 has a Word Search of Glossary Words relating to the winged bugs.

On Pages 55 to 61 there are butterflies flying above big flowers with patterns on their petals to color.

On Pages 63 to 69 there individual large flowers to color.

Page 70 has clues for a Crossword Puzzle that needs you to name the activity a winged bug is doing in this book.

Page 72 has clues for a Crossword Puzzle that needs you to name the type of bug that is named there.

Page 74 has clues for a Crossword Puzzle that needs you to name the winged bug that is engaged in one of the activities described there.

On Pages 77 to 85 are mandalas based on images of flowers and butterflies to color.

Pages 89 to 99 have the Solutions for the Mazes.

Page 102 has the Solution for the Winged Bugs Names Word Search.

Page 103 has the Solution for the Winged Bugs Glossary Word Search.

Page 105 has the Solution for the Winged Bugs Activities Crossword Puzzle.

Page 107 has the Solution for the Winged Bugs Glossary Crossword Puzzle.

Page 109 has the Solution for the Winged Bugs Names Crossword Puzzle.

Pages 110 and 111 there are some book suggestions that kids who love Nature might enjoy.

On Pages 112 and 113 there are some interesting facts about Butterflies and Caterpillars.

Pages 115, 117, 119 and 121 offers places for budding writers to "Write a Story" about their favorite winged bug or butterfly they found in this book.

Pages 114, 116, 118 and 120 have spaces for aspiring artists to draw images relating to the story they wrote or create a new illustration of a winged Bug or butterfly in a different environment.

Frankie Firefly is getting ready to deliver a new light bulb to his friends so they can light up their home again.

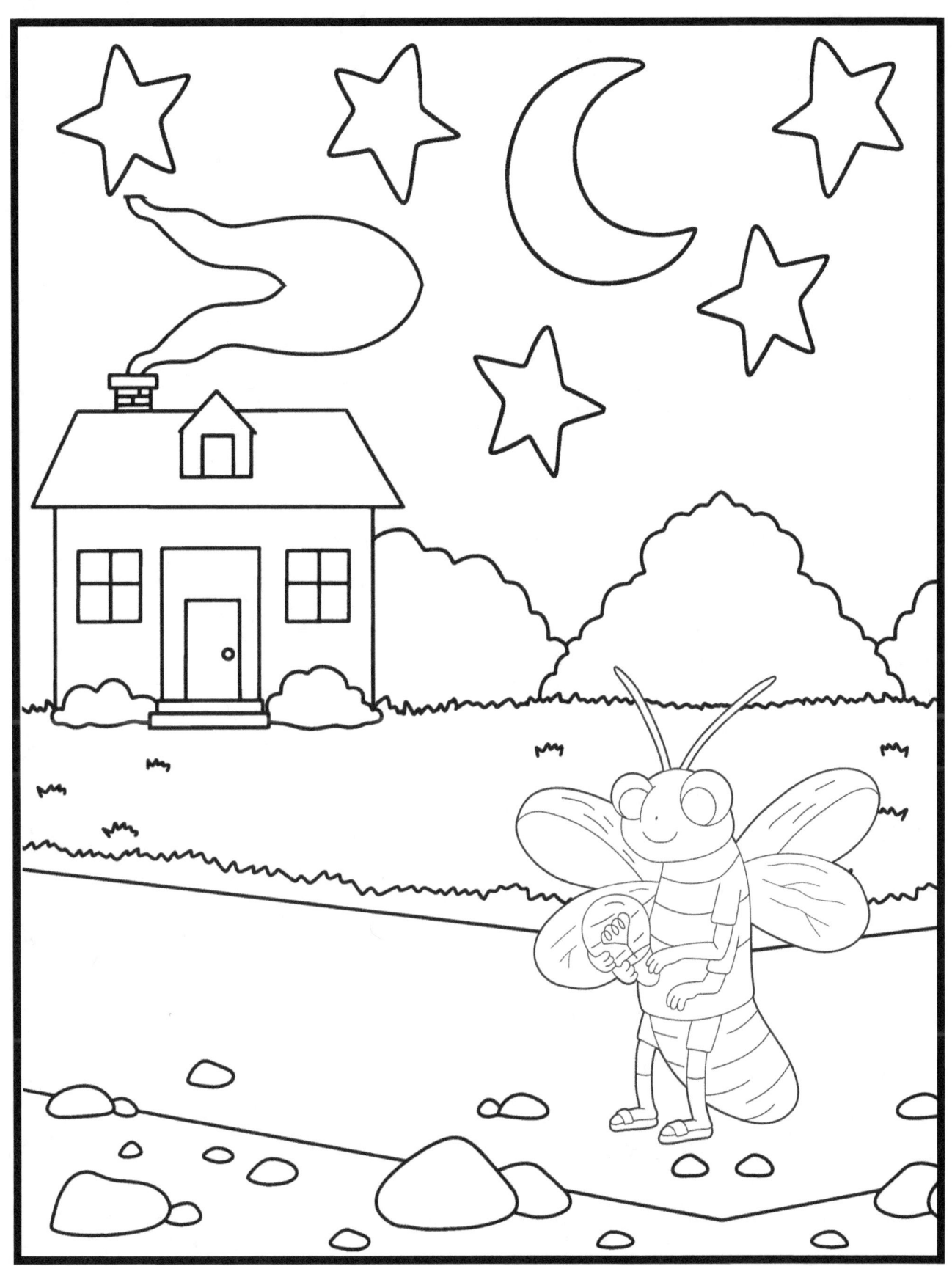

Derrick is a very busy dragonfly who is looking for the house with the address on the note in his hand.

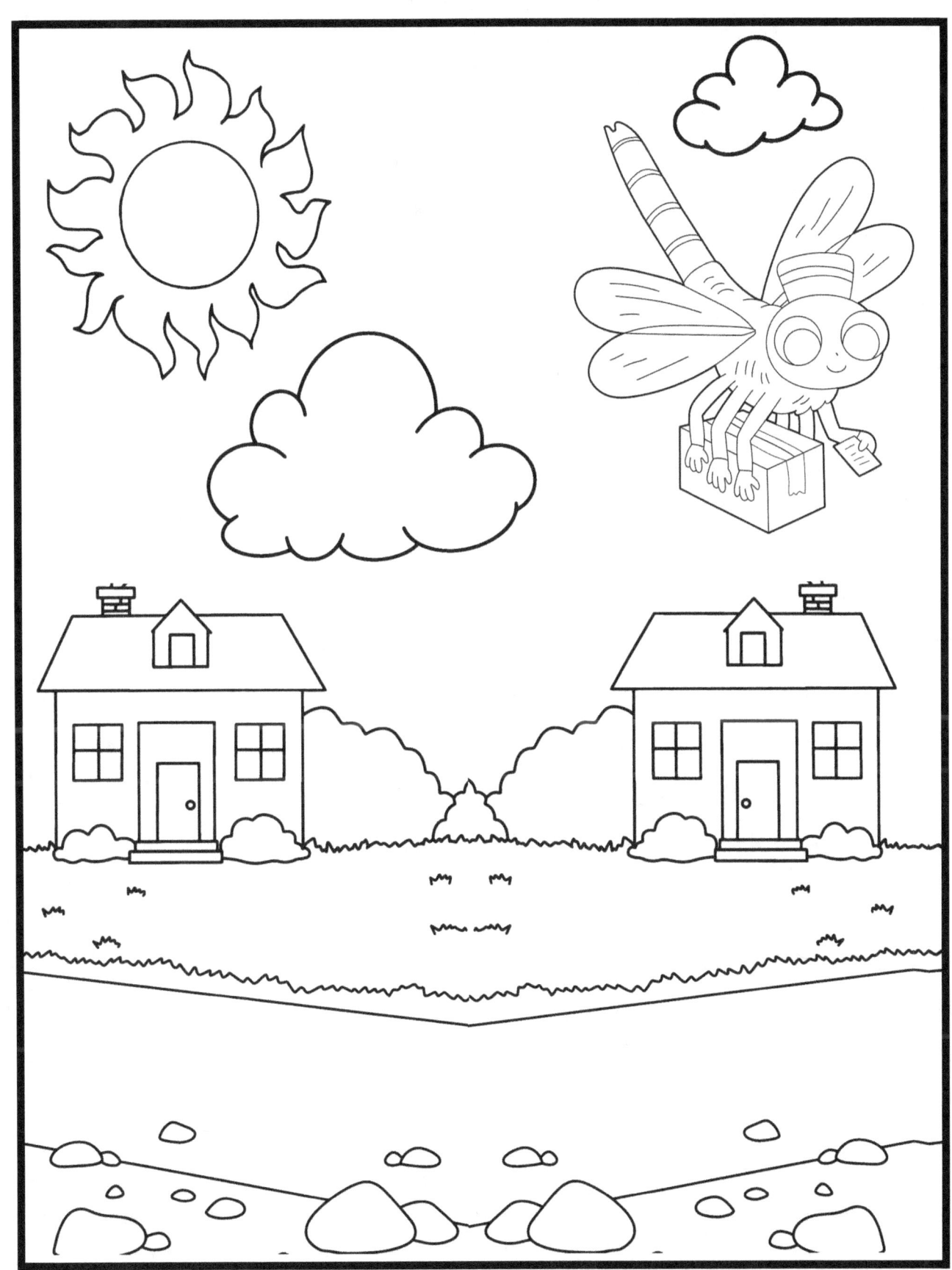

These twin sister bees, **Brandy** and **Brianna**,
need your help painting this fence.

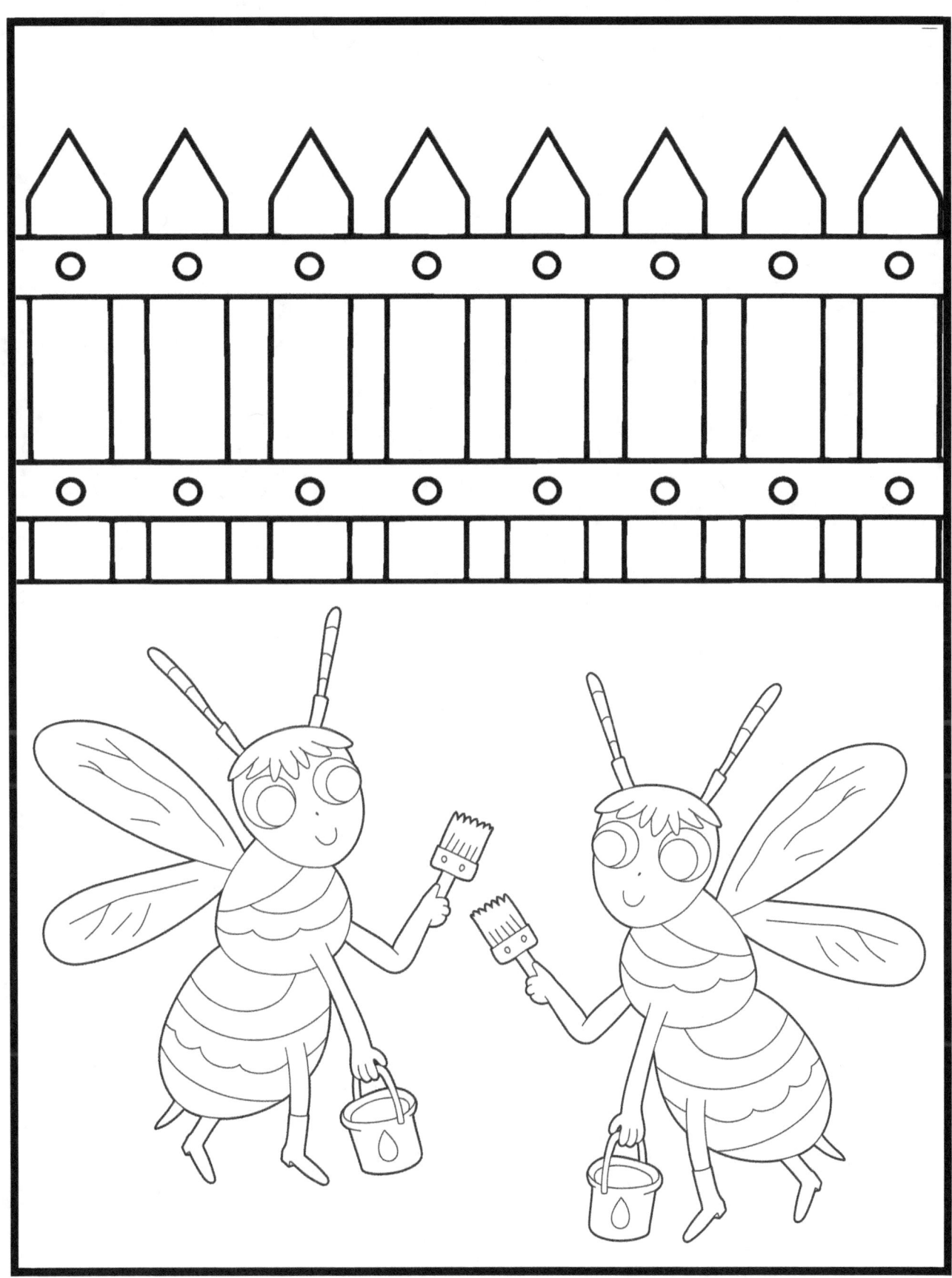

Freddie Fly is enjoying eating his lunch while sitting on a pile of hay bales in front of the farmer's barn.

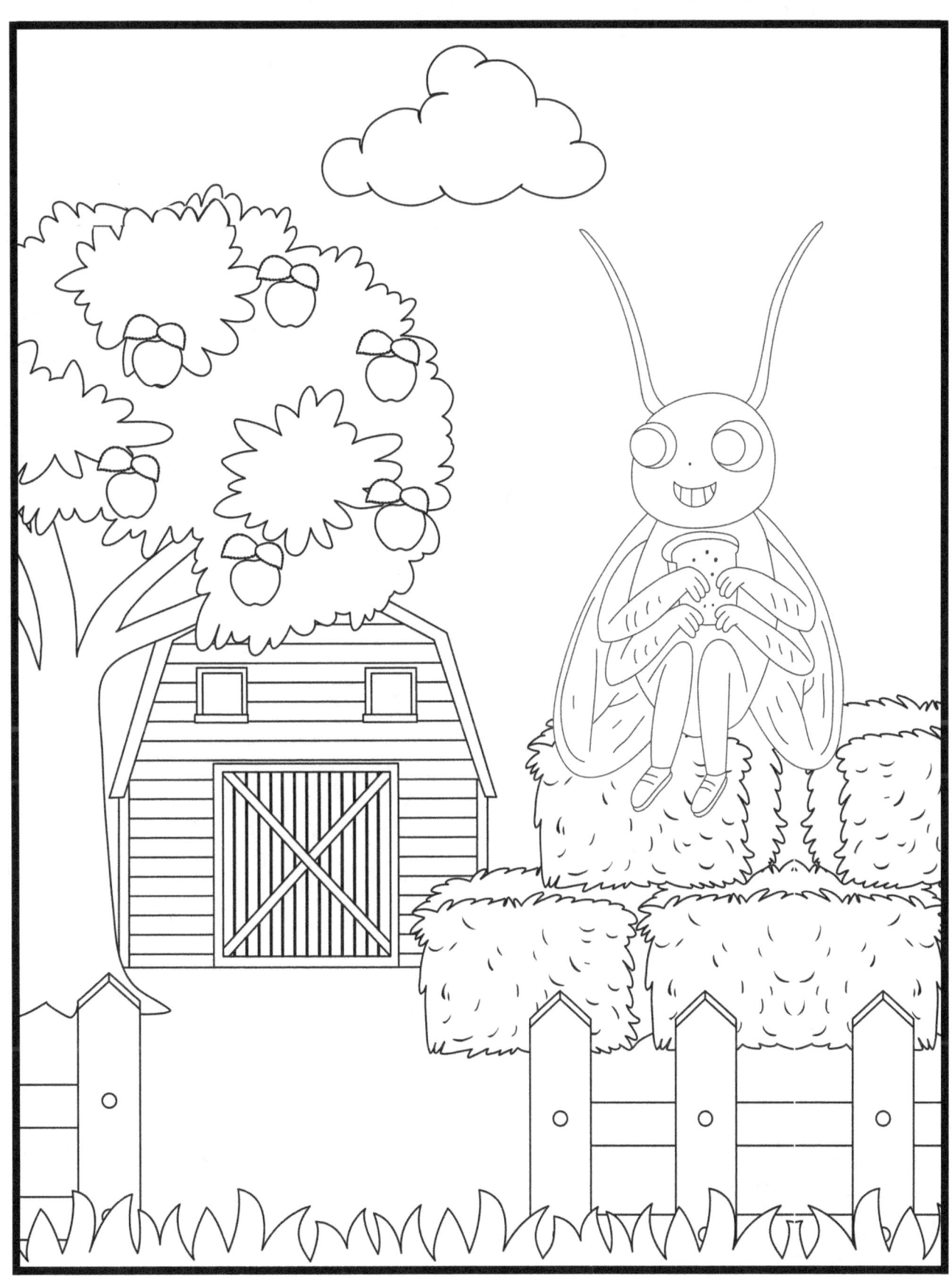

14

Betsy Bumble Bee is enjoying wandering on a path through a field filled with flowers.

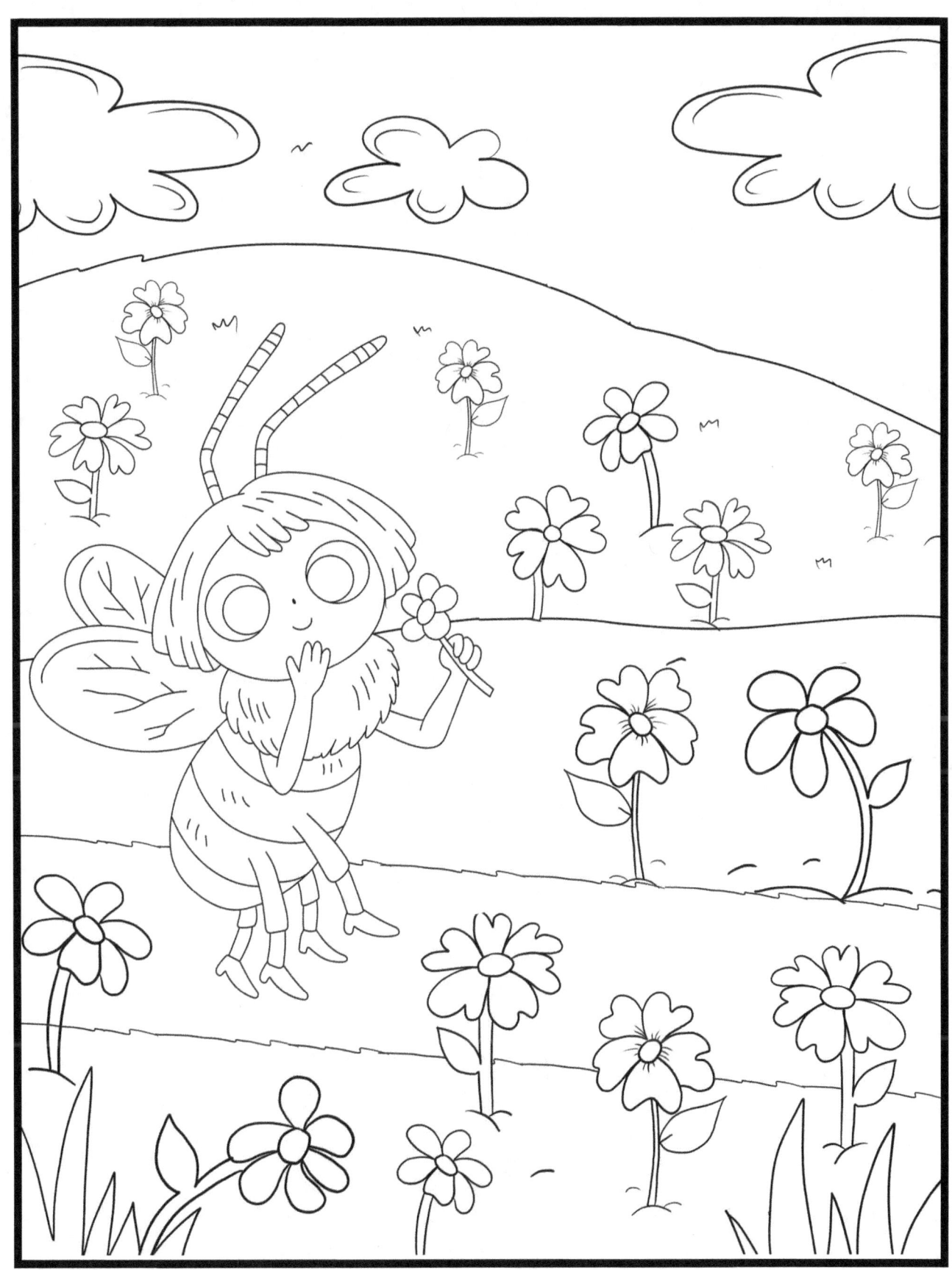

Laci and **Layrue** are two ladybugs who are having
a lazy summer day conversation when they met up
on a pair of big leafy vines that are floating in the air.

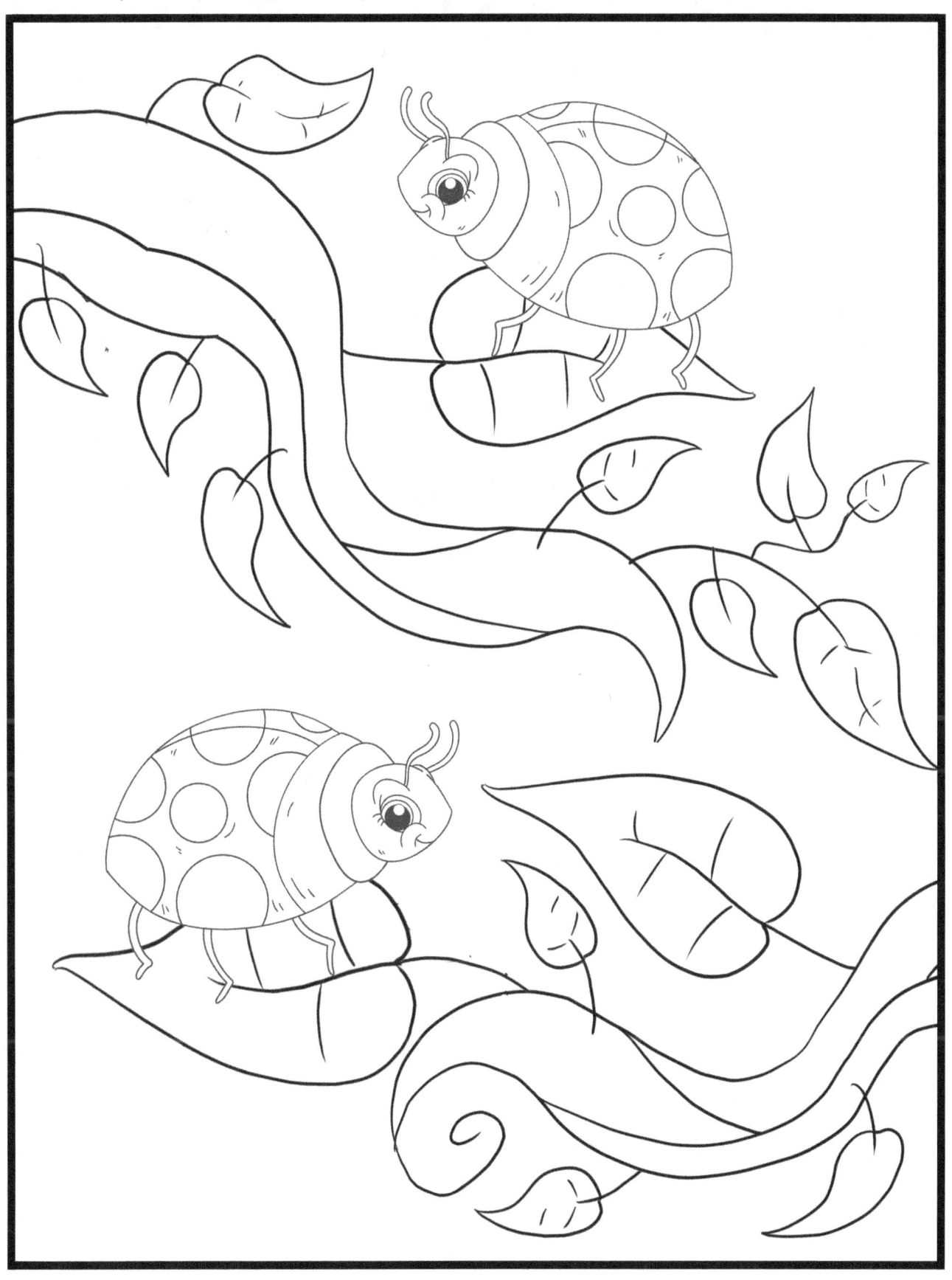

Derrick Dragonfly has finally found the right house to deliver this package to today.

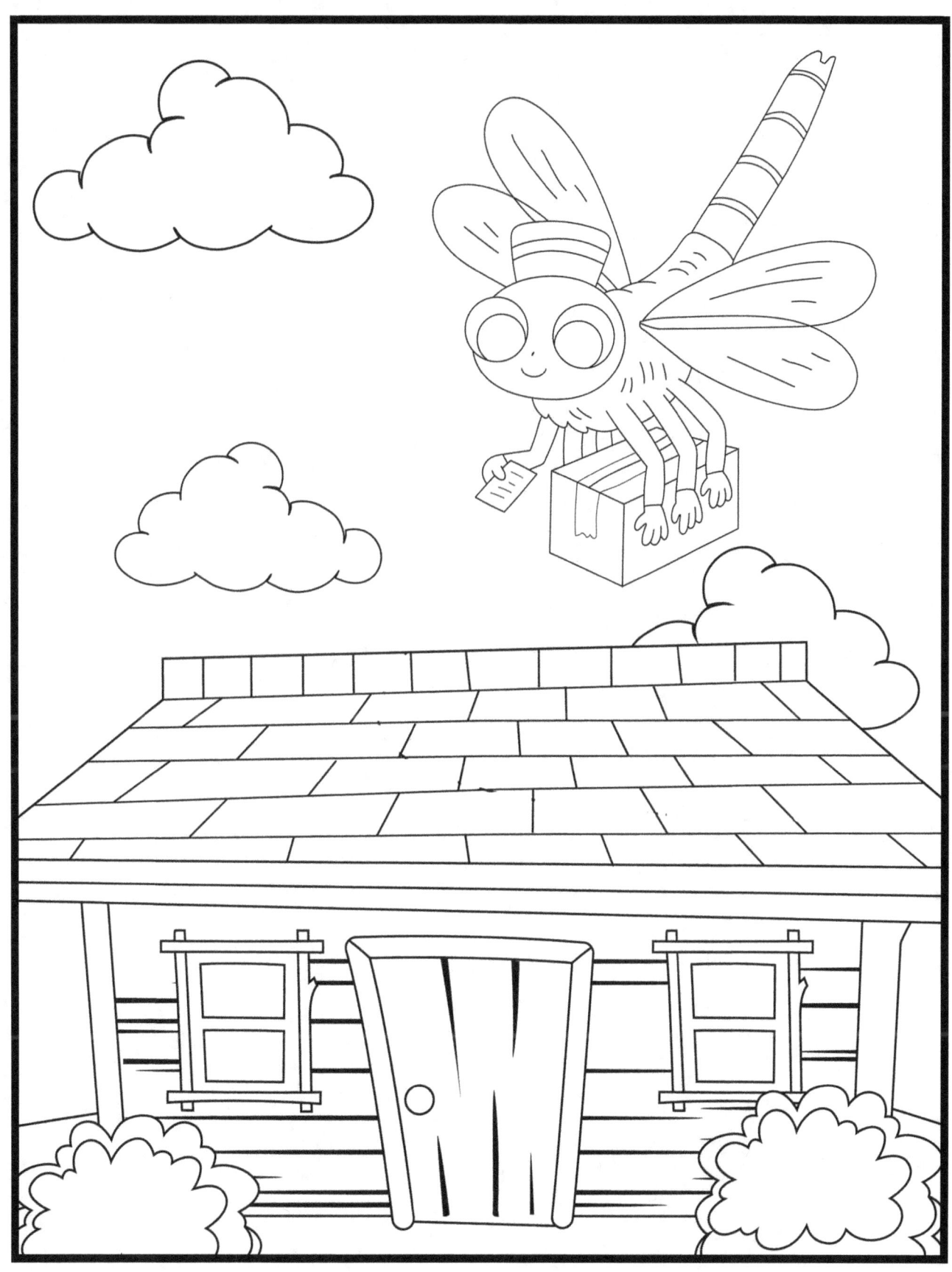

Lizbeth is a very happy butterfly flying under a colorful rainbow above some very large flowers.

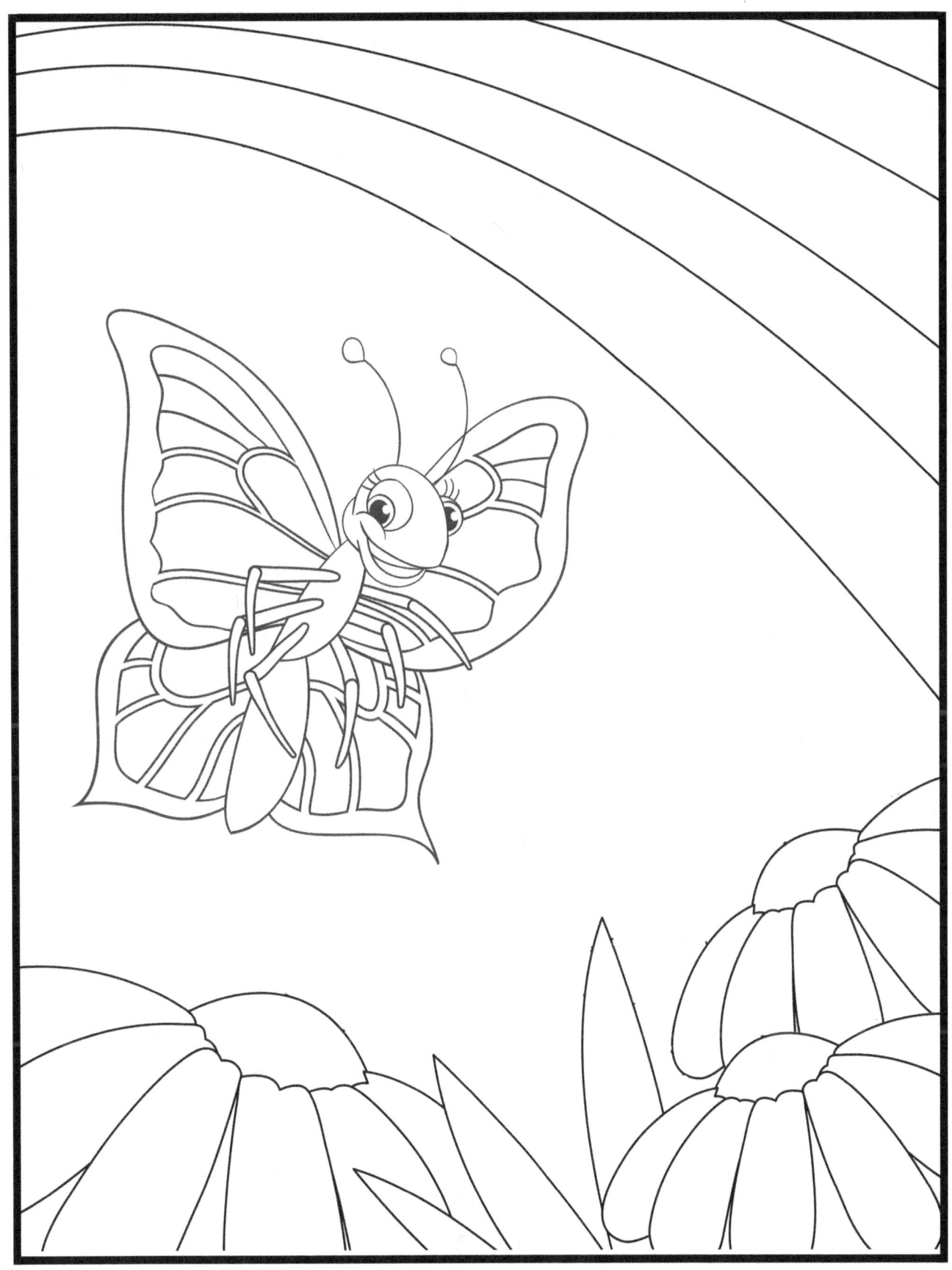

Three smiling butterflies are floating above
some lovely daisy flowers in a beautiful garden.

Three spotted butterflies are flying under a
cloudy sky above a field of little flowers.

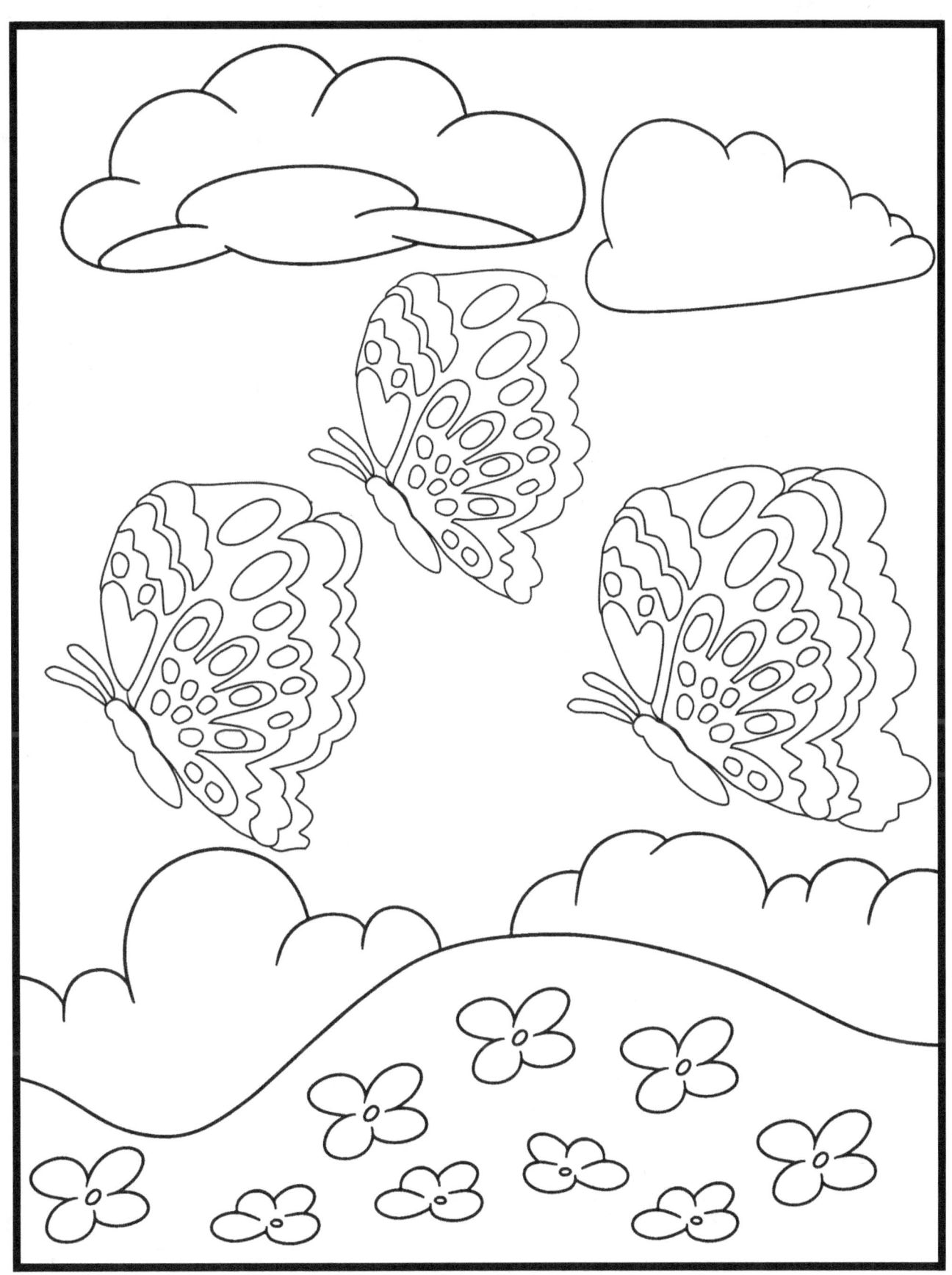

Three butterflies with feathery patterned wings are joyfully flying above a garden of beautiful flowers.

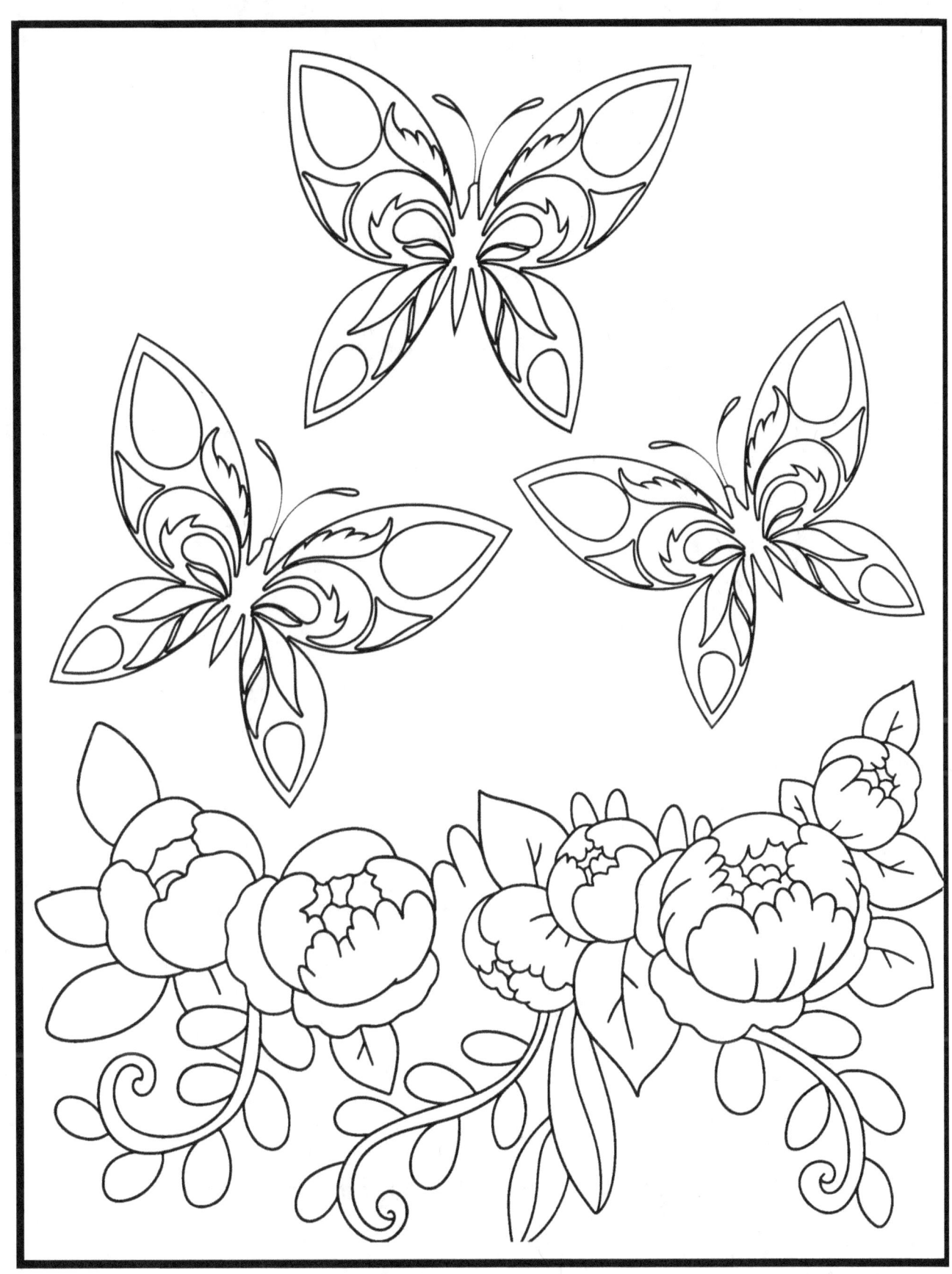

You can find the Solution to this maze on page 89.

A lovely butterfly needs your help to find the path
to beautiful flowers to visit and help pollinate.

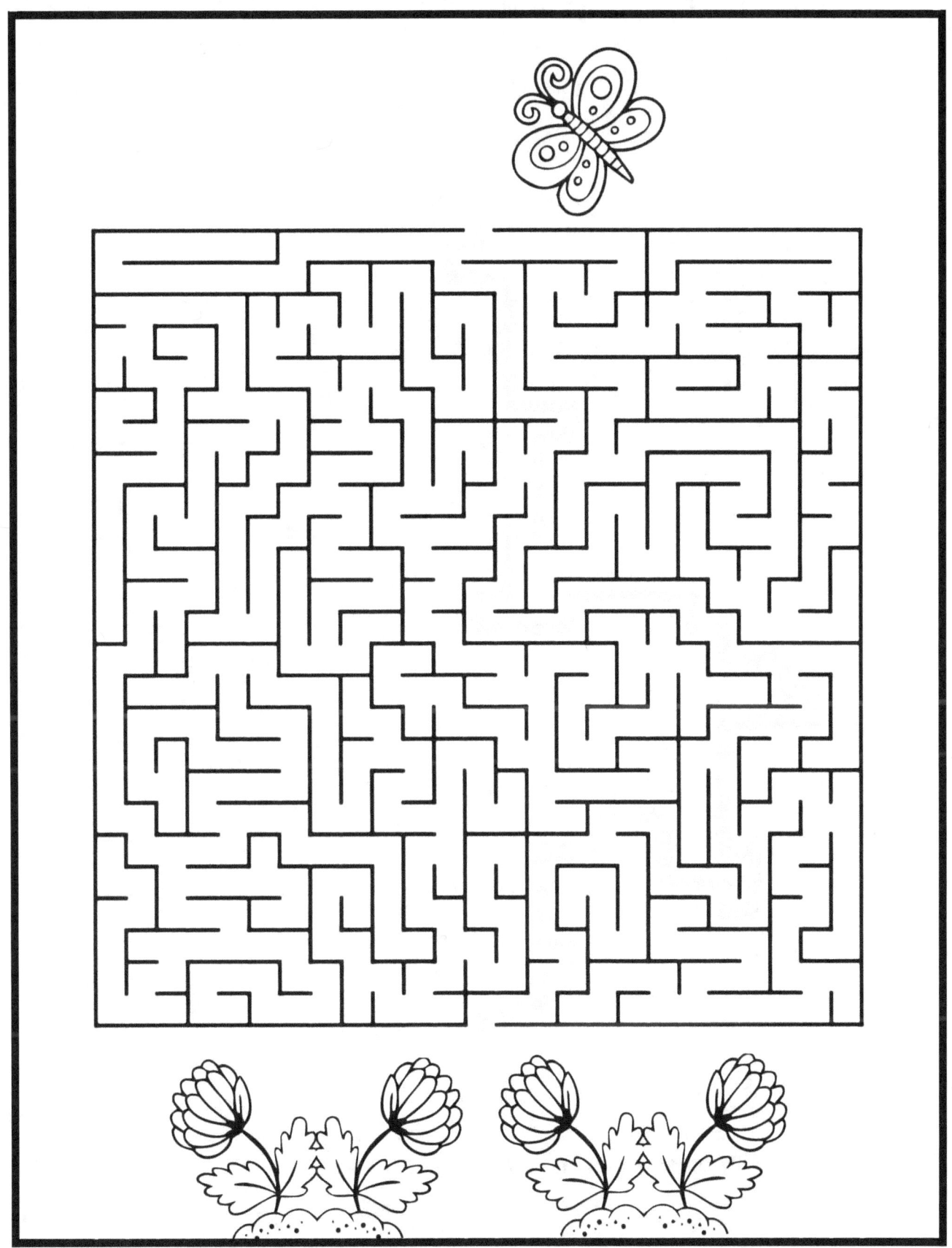

You can find the Solution to this maze on page 91.

A lovely butterfly needs your help to find the path
to beautiful flowers to visit and help pollinate.

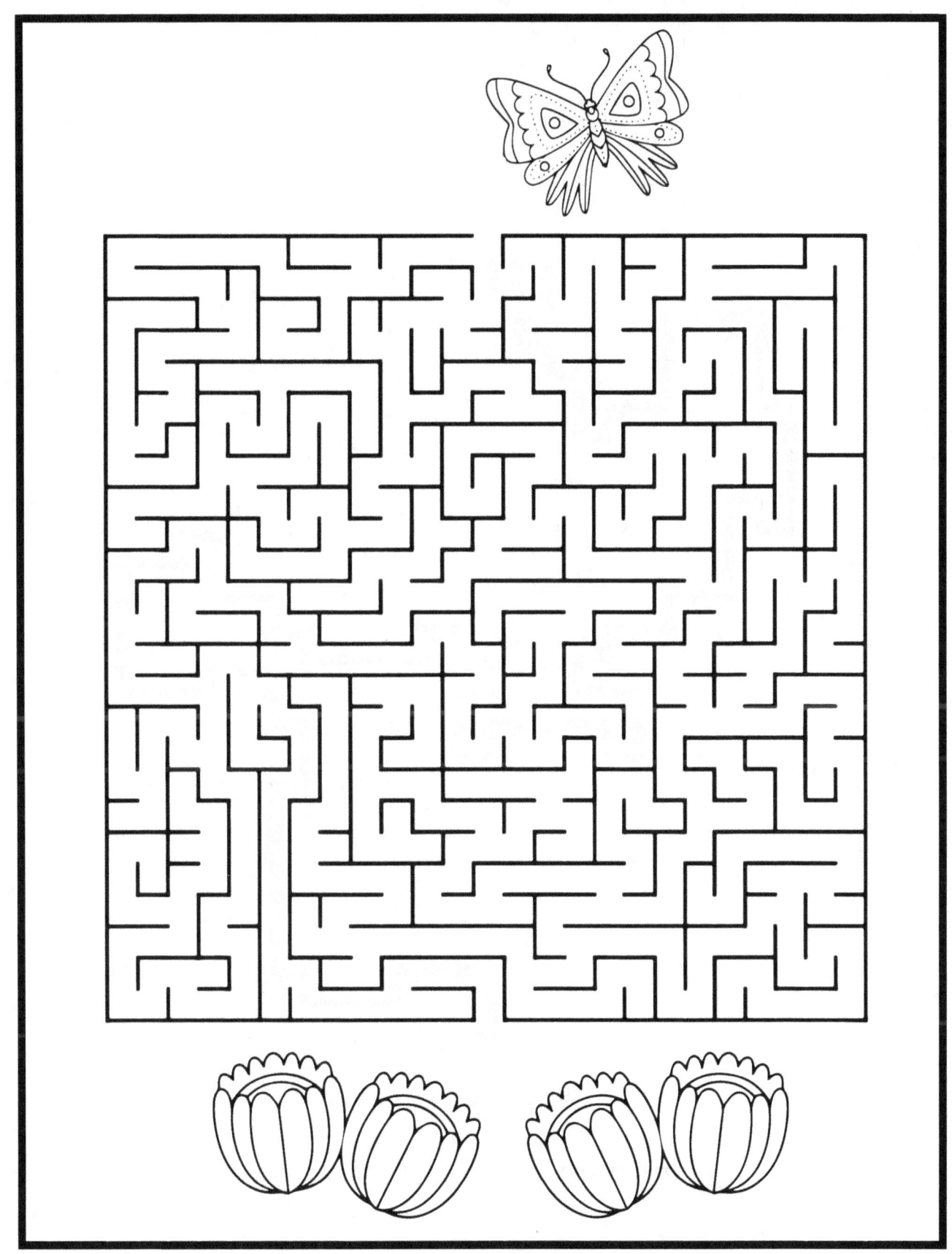

You can find the Solution to this maze on page 93.

A lovely butterfly needs your help to find the path
to beautiful flowers to visit and help pollinate.

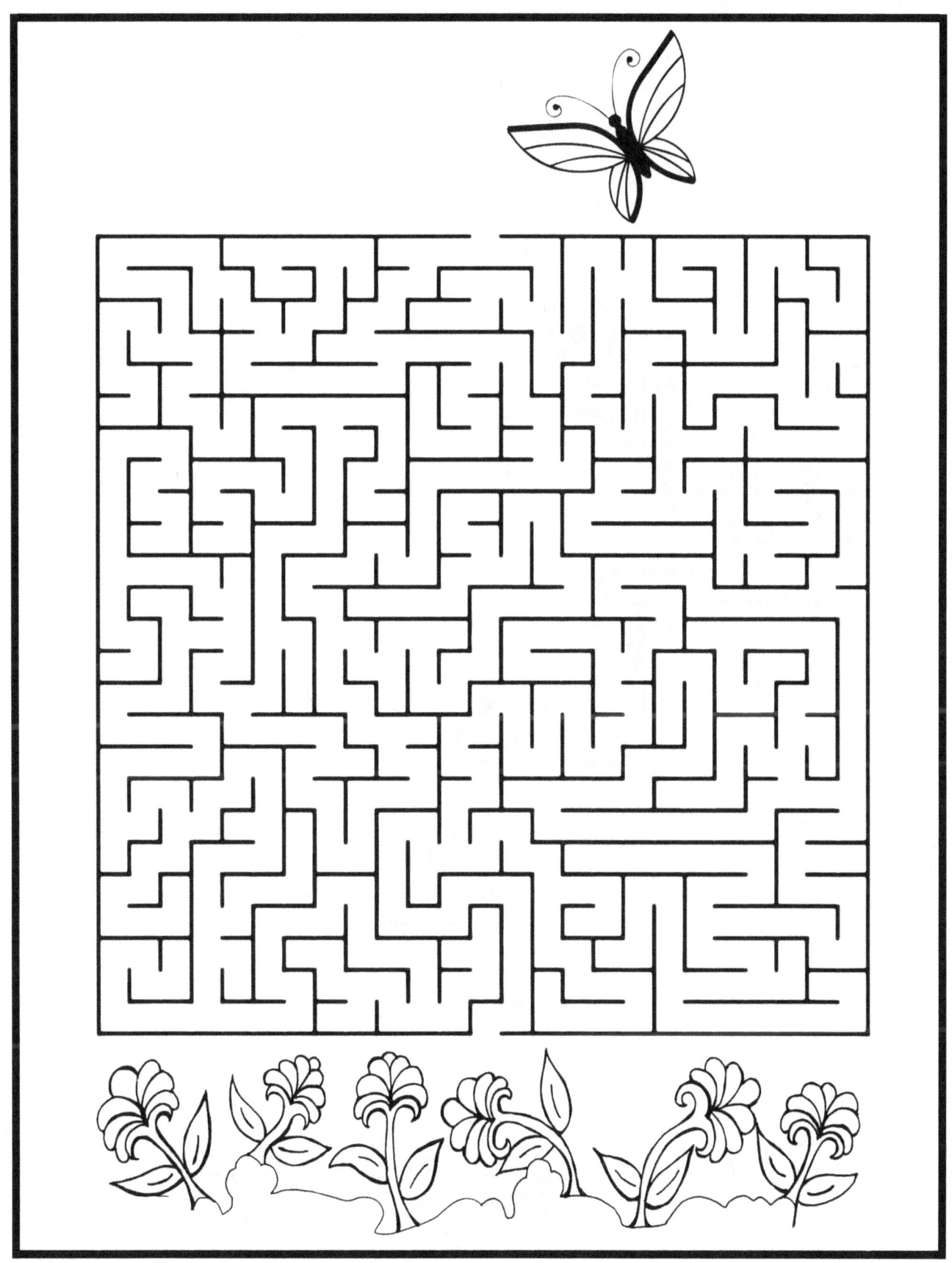

You can find the Solution to this maze on page 95.

A lovely butterfly needs your help to find the path
to beautiful flowers to visit and help pollinate.

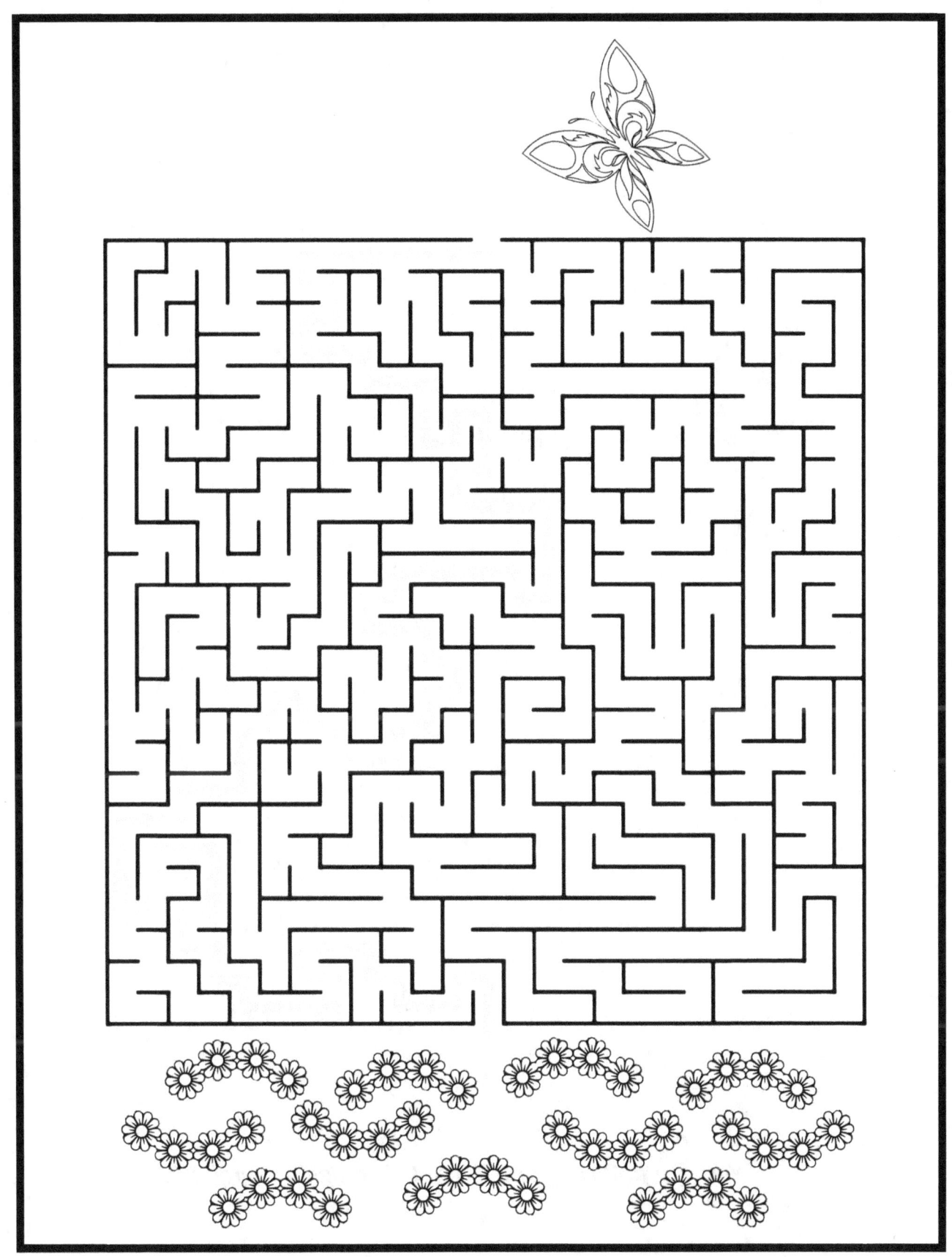

You can find the Solution to this maze on page 97.

A lovely butterfly needs your help to find the path
to beautiful flowers to visit and help pollinate.

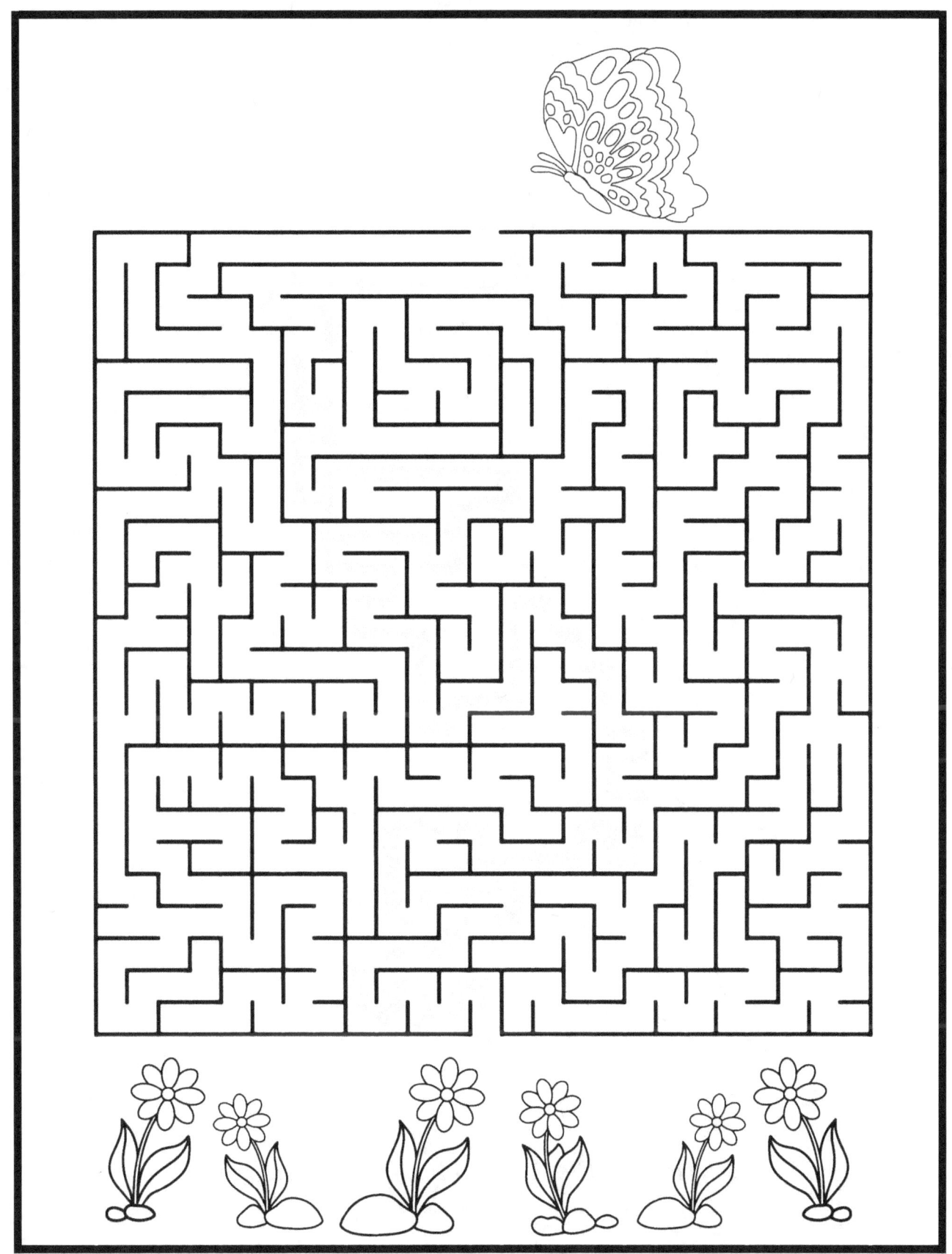

You can find the Solution to this maze on page 99.

A lovely butterfly needs your help to find the path to beautiful flowers to visit and help pollinate.

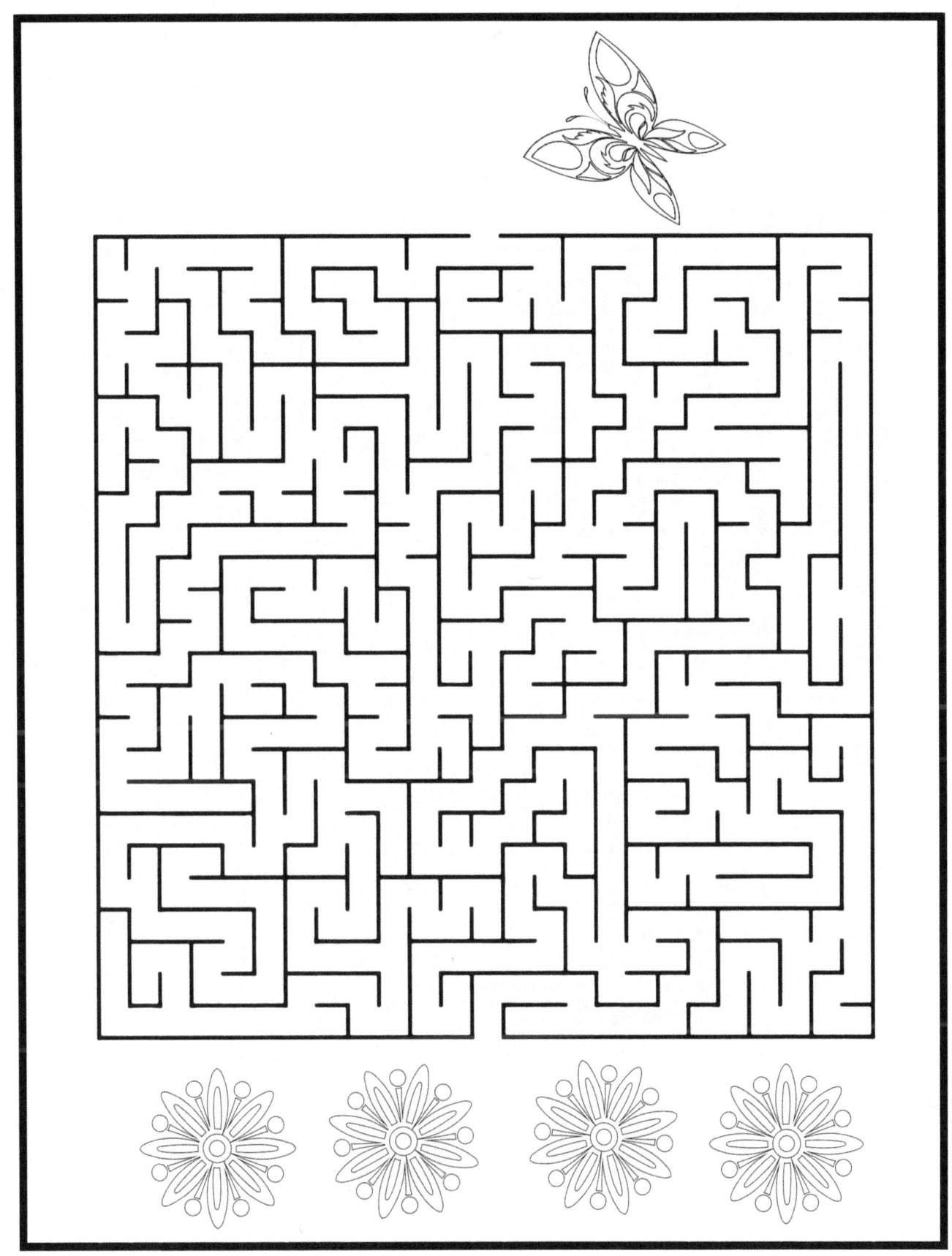

Moki Mosquito is conducting musical flying insects
in a grassy field to share music with his
fun-loving bug friends living there.

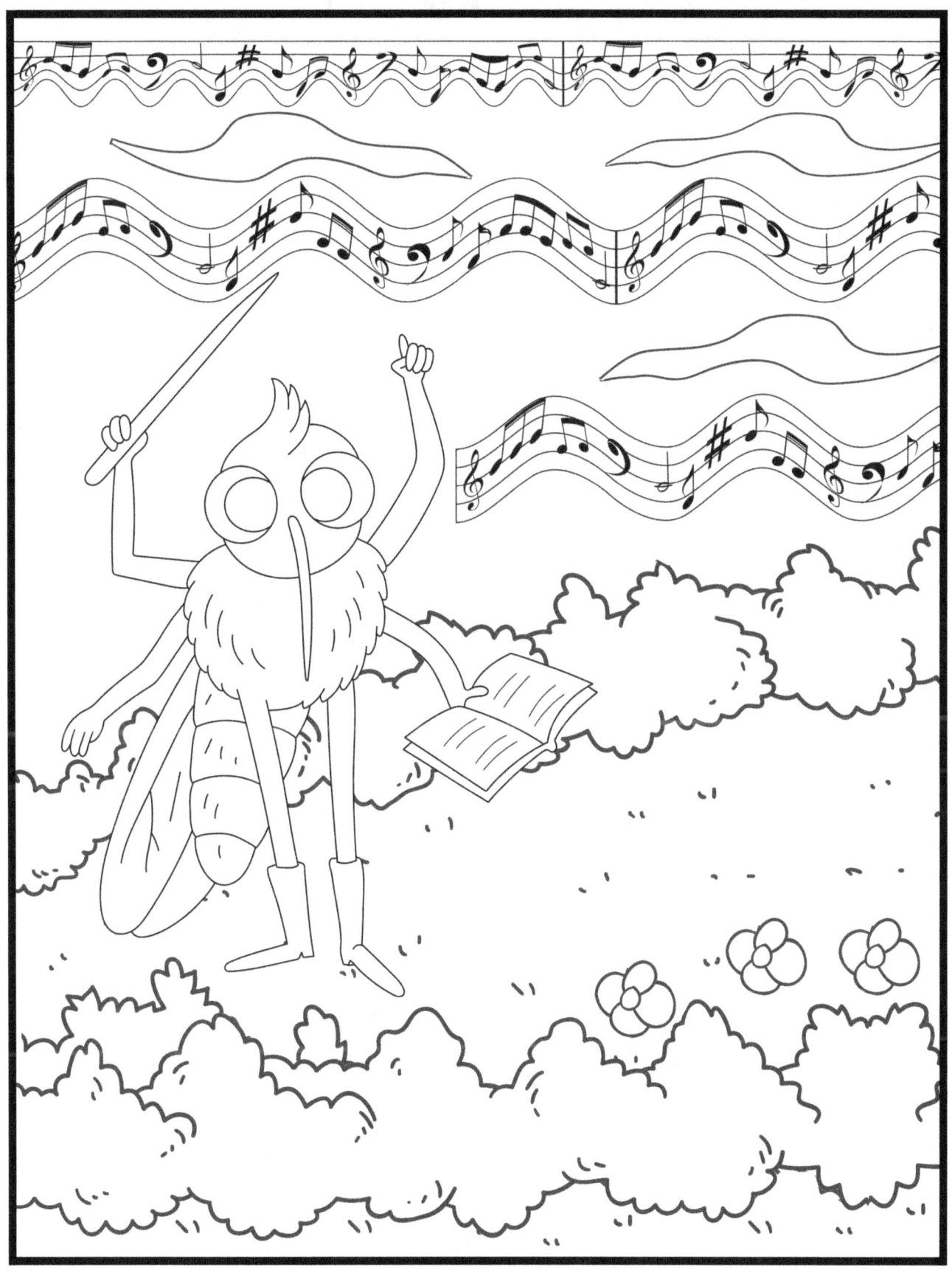

Lovely **Layla** is a green beetle standing on a branch while playing a guitar in the orchestra that is sharing music to entertain their friends that are listening and dancing to it.

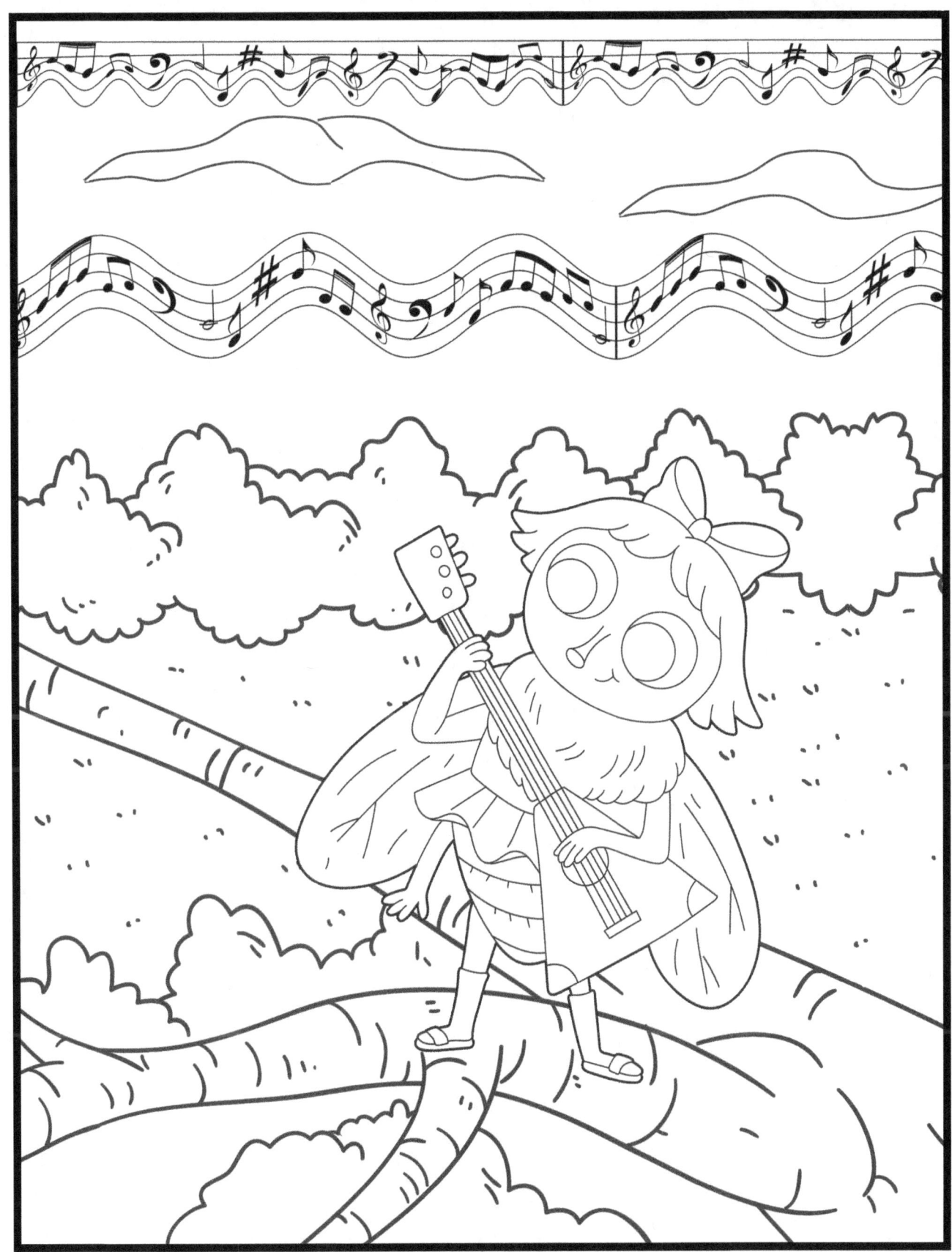

Cecyla is a fun-loving rain beetle enjoying the music she is hearing and dancing on a beautiful big flower blooming on the edge of the grassy field.

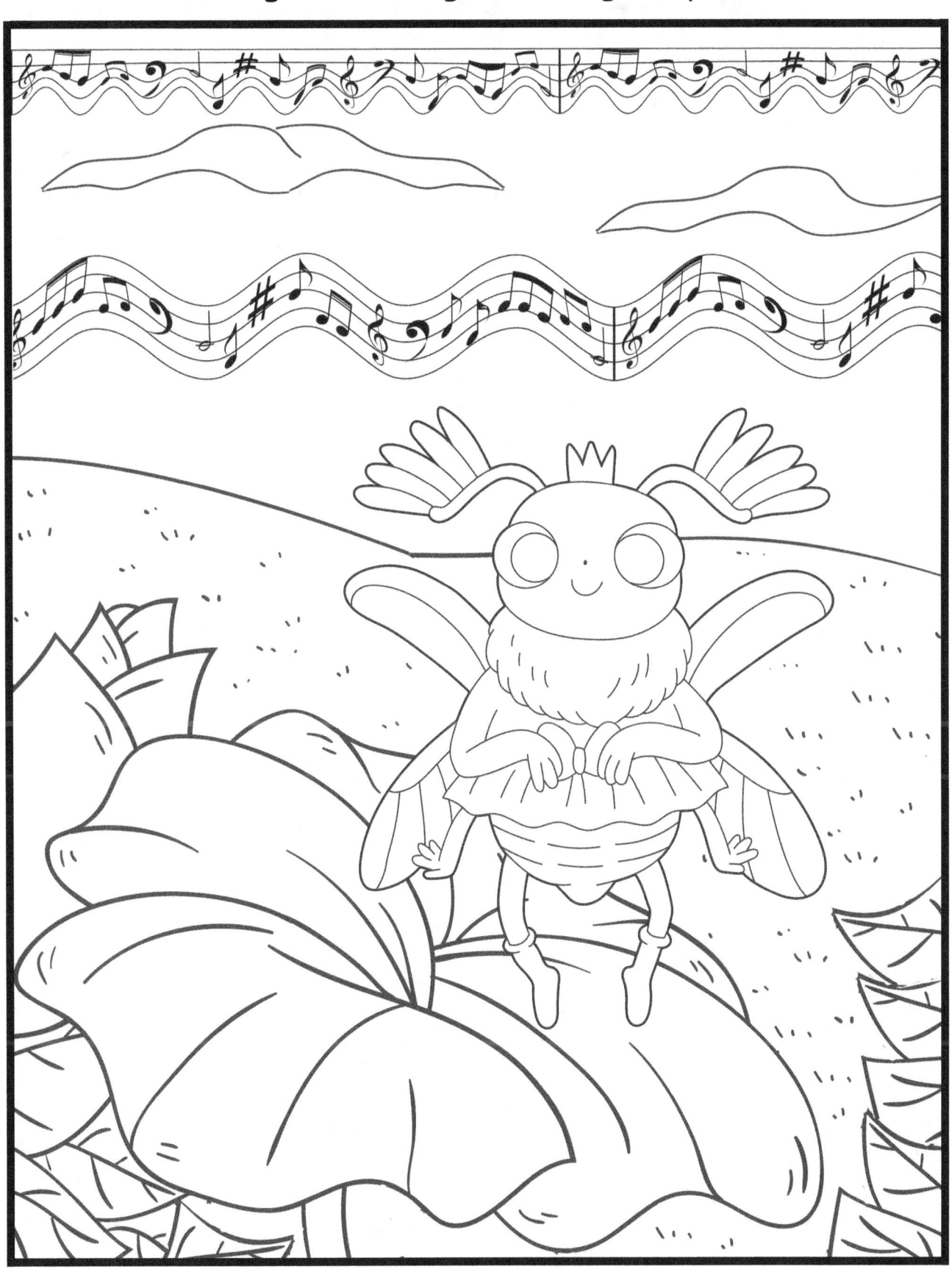

46

Beette Beetle is playing many instruments to add rhythm to the music the flying creatures band is playing on a warm summer day.

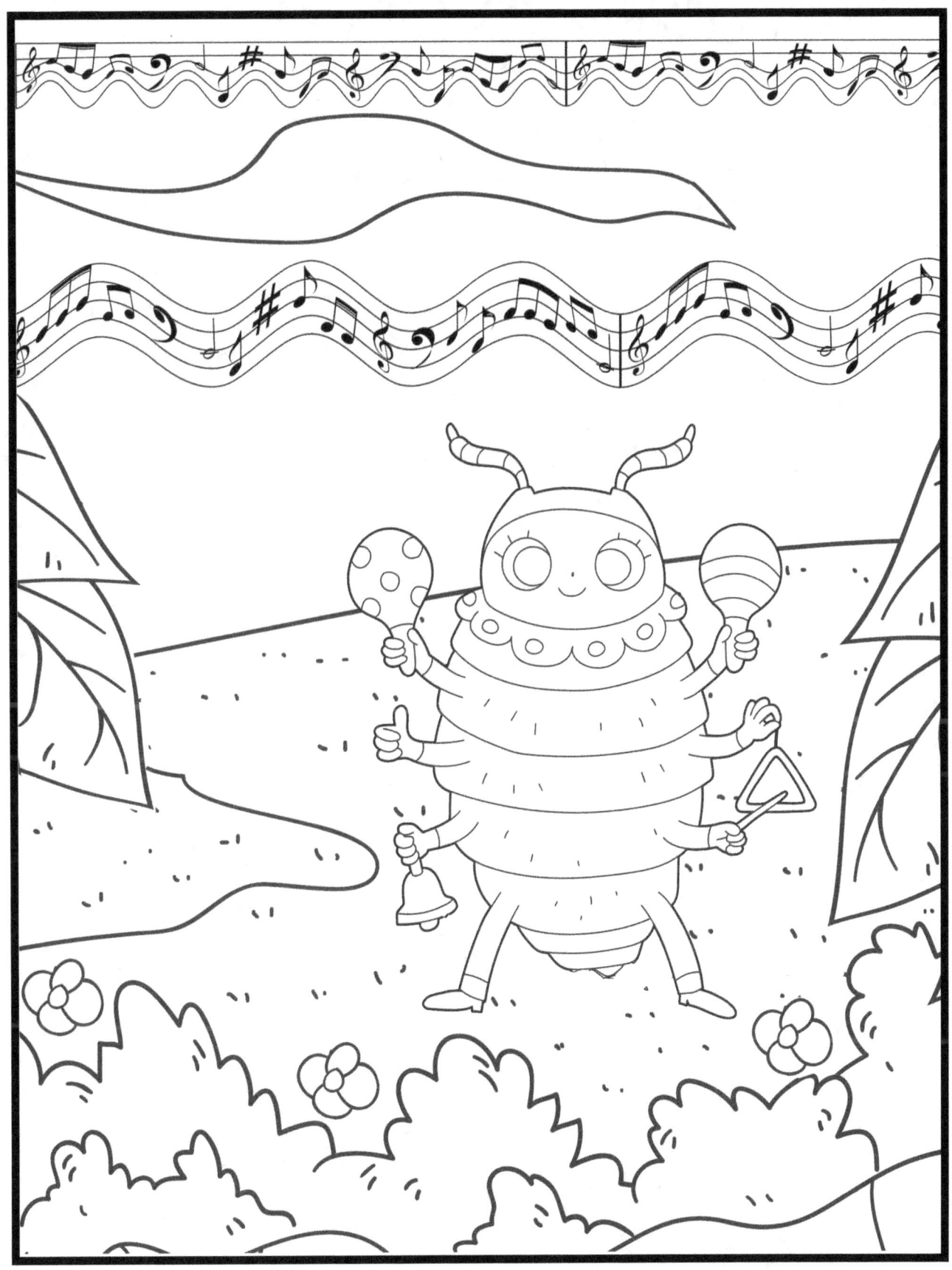

Two lovely grasshoppers, **Gracie** and her sister **Gaga**
are having fun dancing to the music floating
in the air above this grassy field.

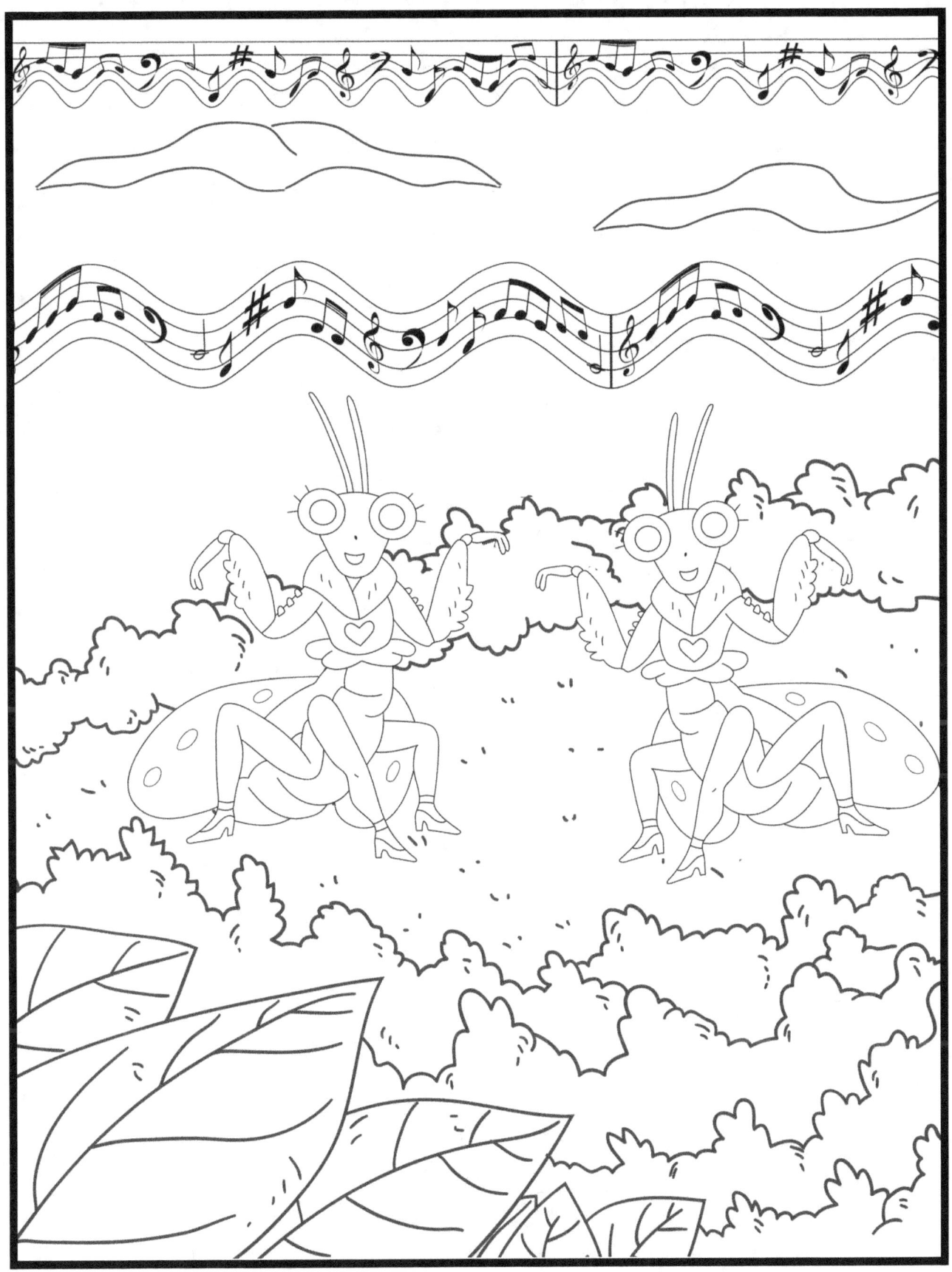

50

Winged Bugs Names Word Search Puzzle.

Circle the words in the list when you find them in the square below.

Mark an X next to each word in the list when you find it.

Find the Solution on page 102.

__ DERRICK	__ BETSY	__ LAYLA
__ BRANDY	__ LACI	__ GRACIE
__ BRIANNA	__ LAYRUE	__ GAGA
__ FREDDIE	__ LIZBETH	__ BEETTE
__ FRANKIE	__ MOKI	__ CECYLA

Z	L	N	S	T	Y	I	E	I	K	N	A	R	F	E
R	T	T	L	I	Z	B	E	T	H	I	K	Z	R	F
T	C	N	J	K	Q	S	D	C	N	Y	L	P	E	H
B	E	E	T	T	E	V	E	W	G	A	N	X	D	M
W	X	Z	C	C	U	J	I	M	B	R	U	Q	D	O
I	Y	O	P	Y	M	N	B	A	C	L	A	C	I	P
E	F	B	M	C	L	T	G	T	L	O	L	C	E	O
O	P	M	J	L	N	A	B	V	A	C	X	Z	I	U
A	F	G	N	H	G	P	C	S	Y	O	D	N	R	E
S	D	Y	S	Y	S	T	E	B	L	A	E	N	E	D
O	F	D	E	N	Y	O	U	D	A	E	D	E	W	S
E	E	N	F	L	D	E	R	R	I	C	K	F	Q	A
D	L	A	Y	E	E	D	Y	D	O	K	N	Y	L	C
O	B	R	I	A	N	N	A	N	F	S	O	D	K	Z
H	I	B	T	S	L	E	L	O	E	D	Y	M	J	M

Winged Bugs Glossary Word Search Puzzle.

Circle the words in the list when you find them in the square below.

Mark an X next to each word in the list when you find it.

Find the Solution on page 103.

__ BEE   __ DRAGONFLY   __ LADYBUG
__ BEETLE   __ FIREFLY   __ MONARCH
__ BUMBLEBEE   __ FLY   __ MOSQUITO
__ BUTTERFLY   __ GRASSHOPPER   __ RAINBEETLE

Z	A	S	D	F	G	H	J	K	L	G	Q	M	W	G
H	E	T	Y	U	M	O	S	Q	U	I	T	O	S	D
D	I	S	A	O	G	C	E	B	B	R	O	N	J	L
C	F	I	R	E	F	L	Y	F	W	P	E	A	T	N
G	R	E	M	R	N	D	X	E	E	B	F	R	K	W
D	E	W	P	Z	A	I	S	V	Z	Q	M	C	A	M
F	P	L	D	L	O	I	D	M	H	N	Y	H	z	B
Y	P	D	R	A	G	O	N	F	L	Y	L	J	E	R
W	O	A	G	J	R	K	M	B	I	N	F	D	H	z
J	H	N	L	E	S	Y	O	Z	E	L	R	U	C	T
R	S	T	Q	B	L	E	K	N	T	E	E	S	Y	X
H	S	P	Z	F	X	R	C	B	E	E	T	L	E	L
U	A	W	S	O	J	I	Y	U	G	Q	T	L	H	K
K	R	V	T	E	E	B	E	L	B	M	U	B	E	D
A	G	F	J	D	H	G	M	R	S	W	B	F	A	Z

Two butterflies with feathery wings are dancing in the sky around a flower with patterns on its petals to color.

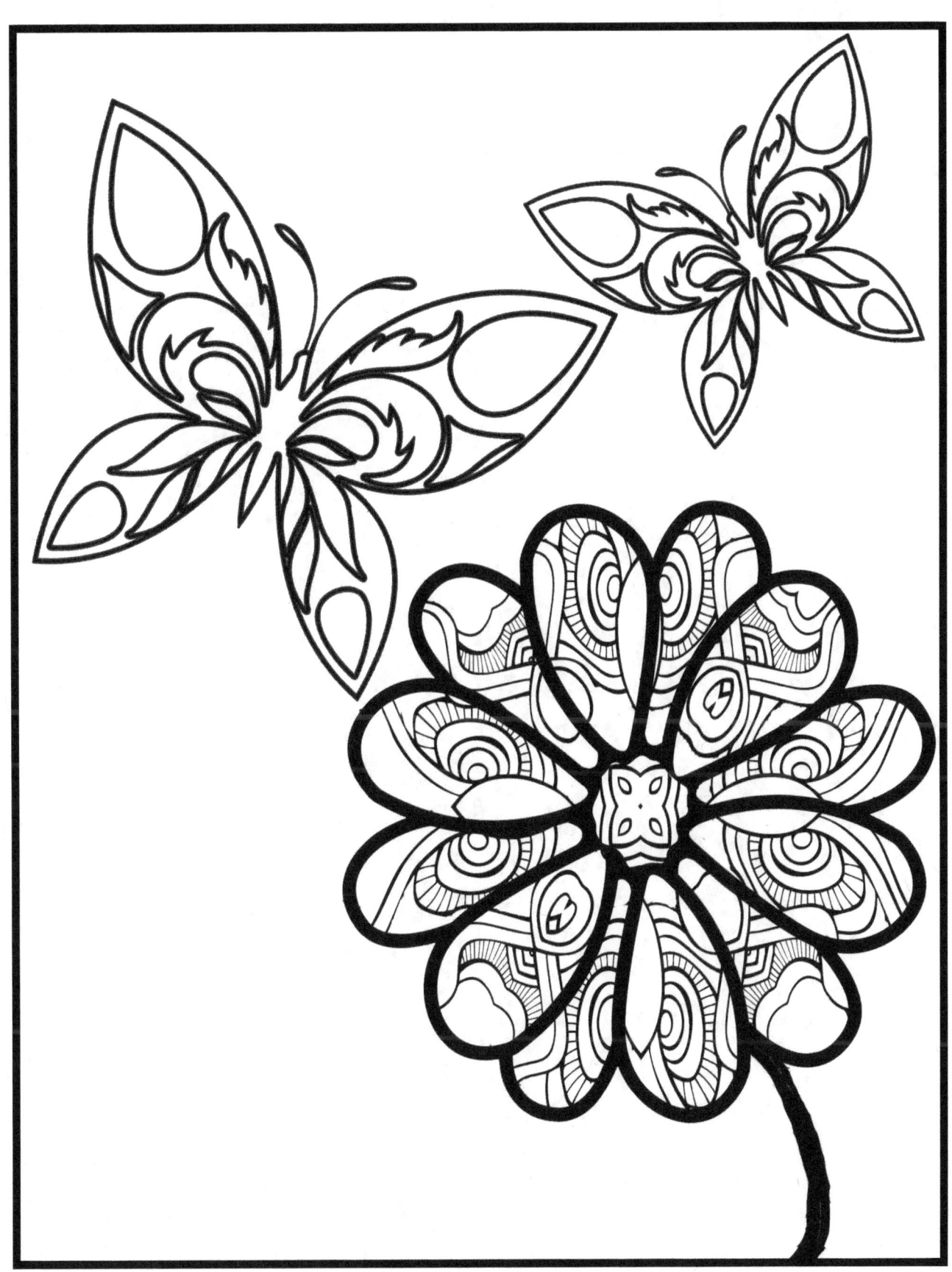

Three Monarch butterflies are floating above
a flower with patterns on its petals to color.

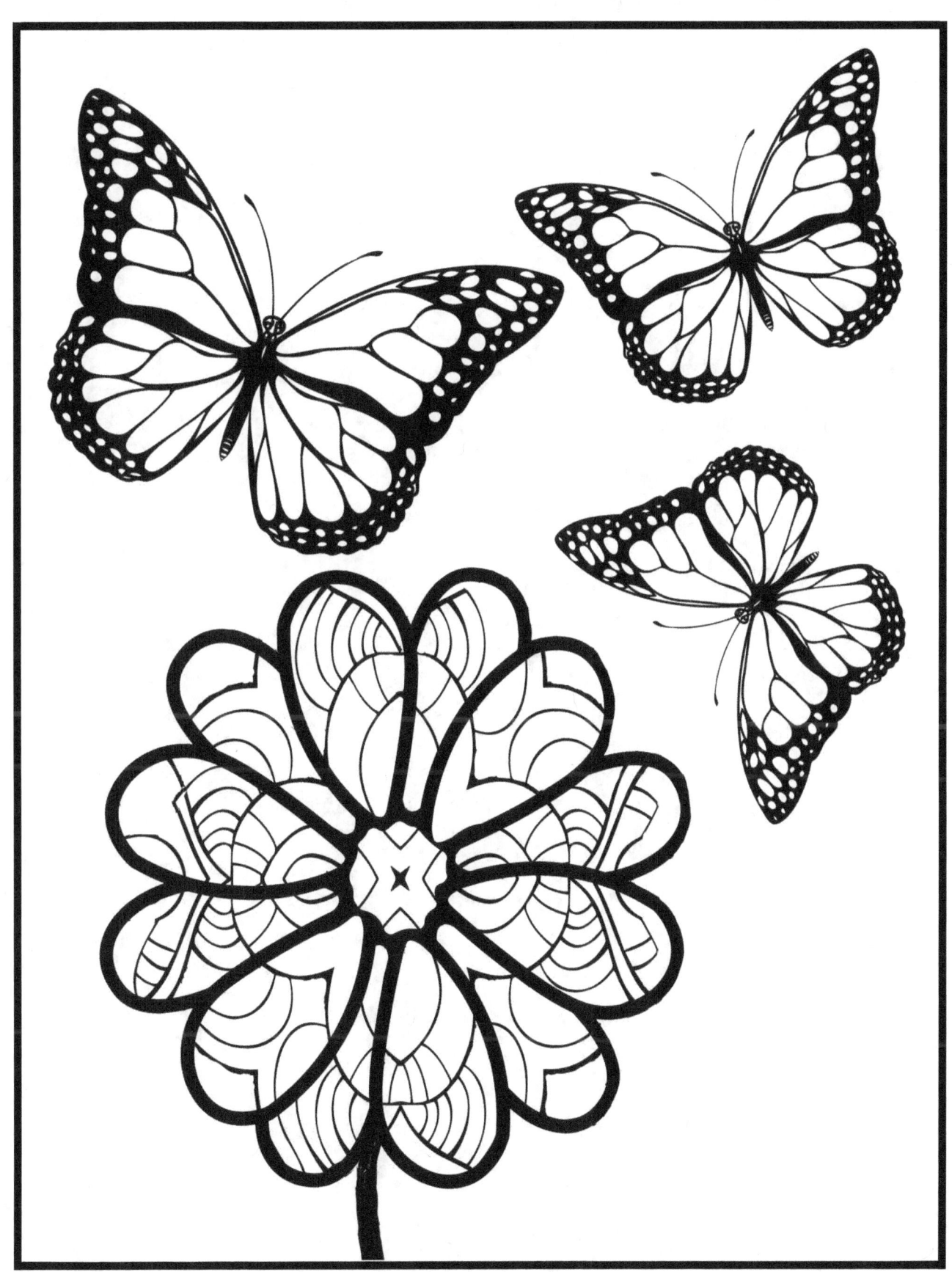

Three lovely butterflies are flying around a flower with heart-based patterns on its petals to color.

A very delicate butterfly is fluttering around
a flower with patterns on its petals to color.

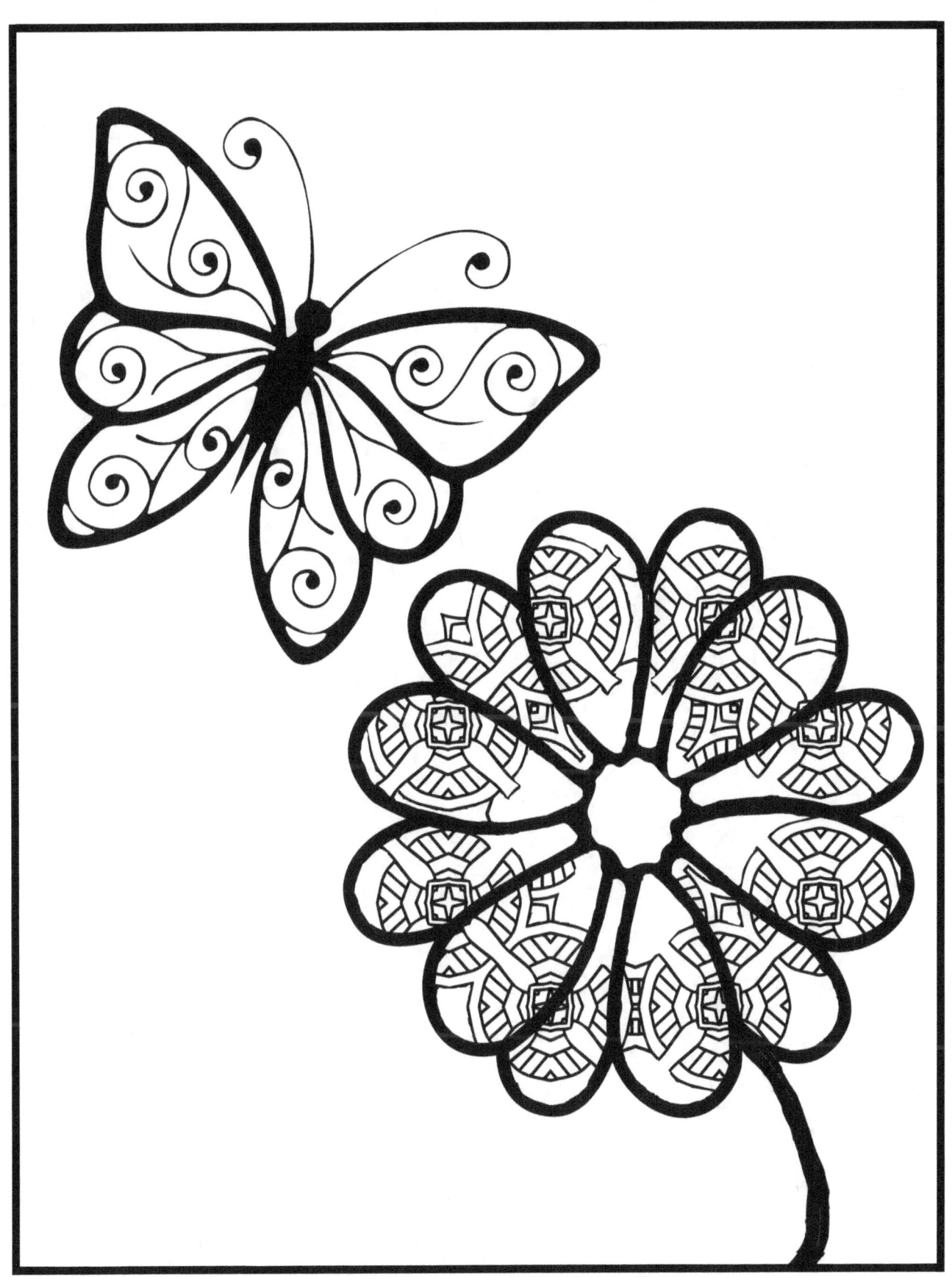

Flower Mandala

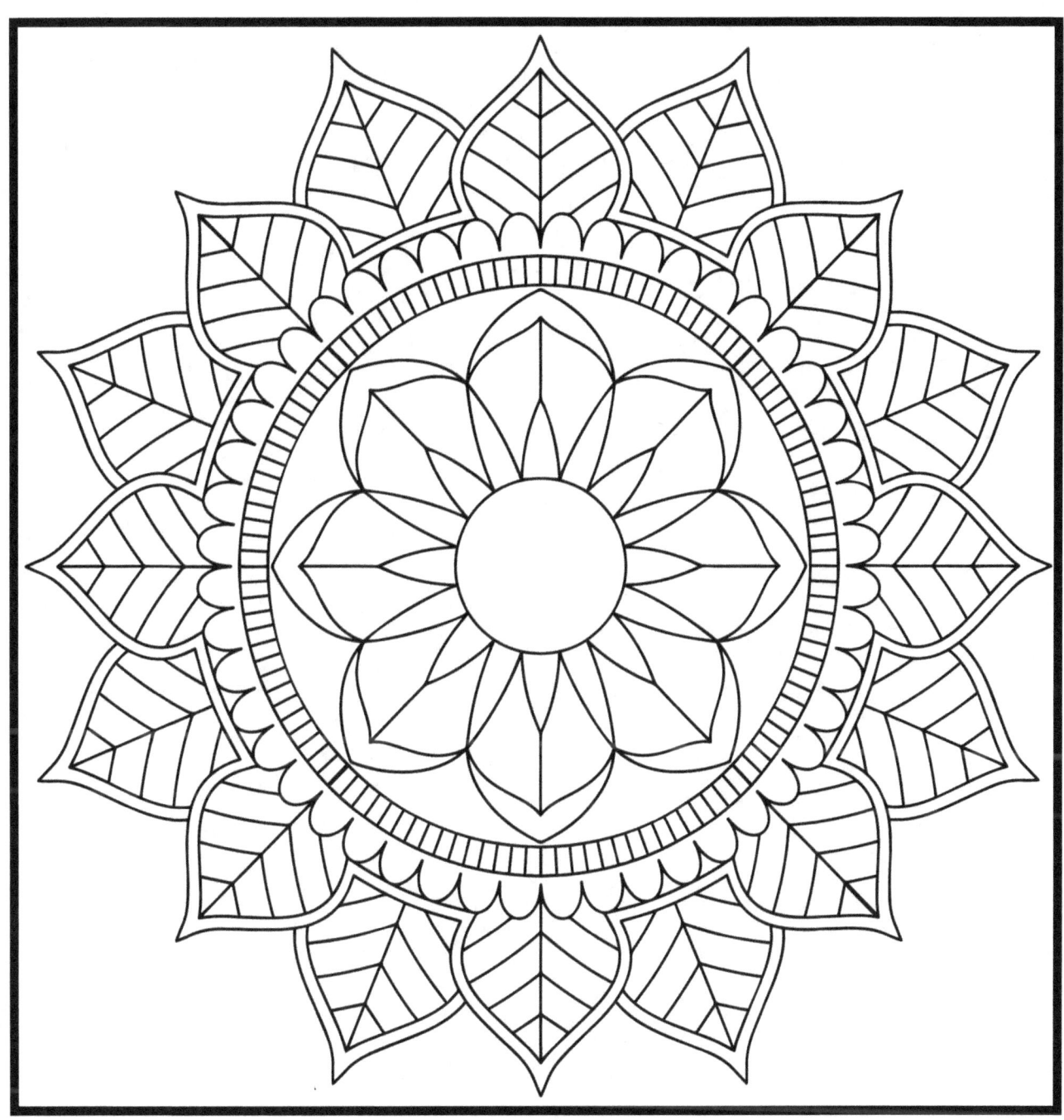

Flower Mandala

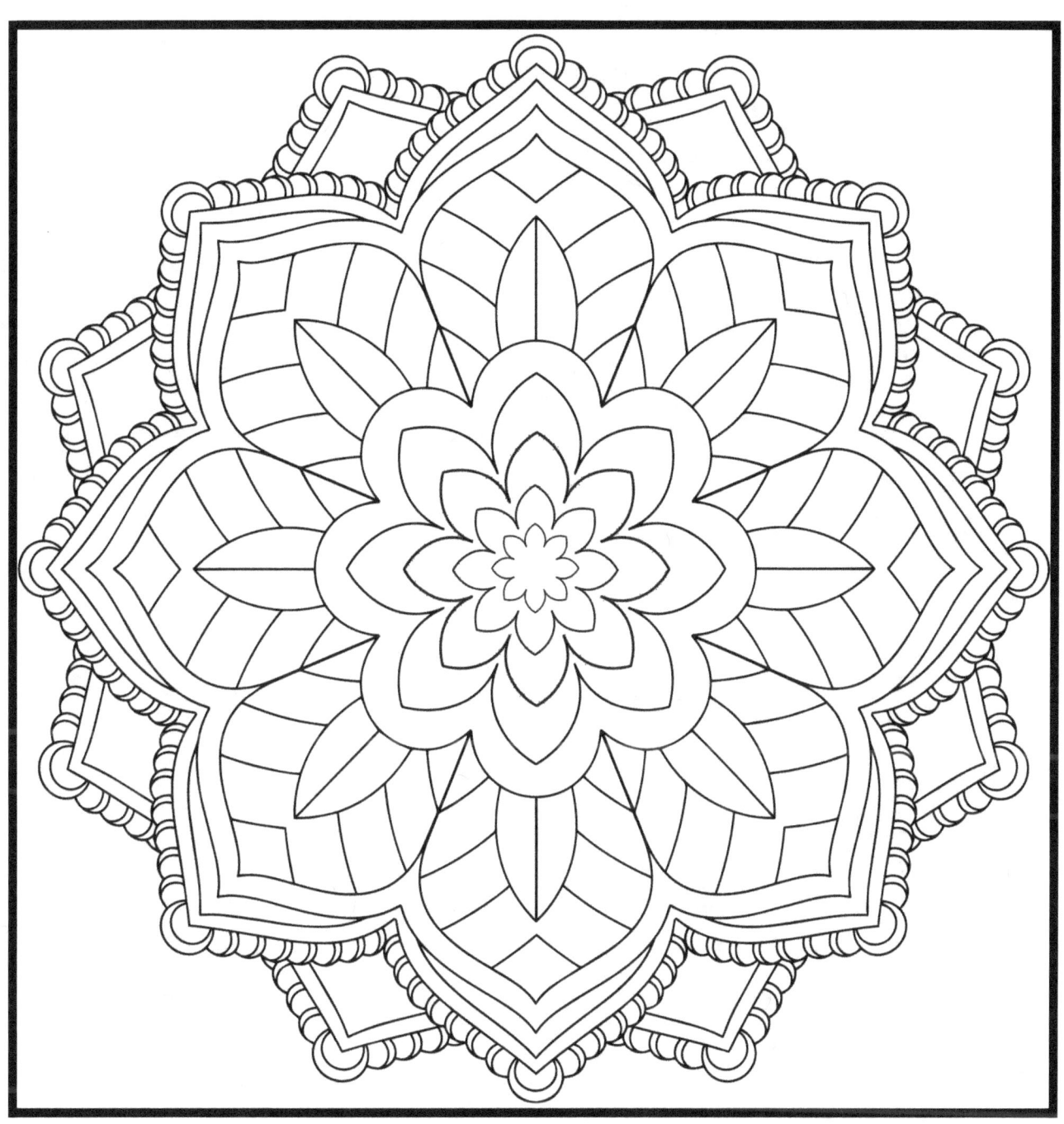

Flower Mandala

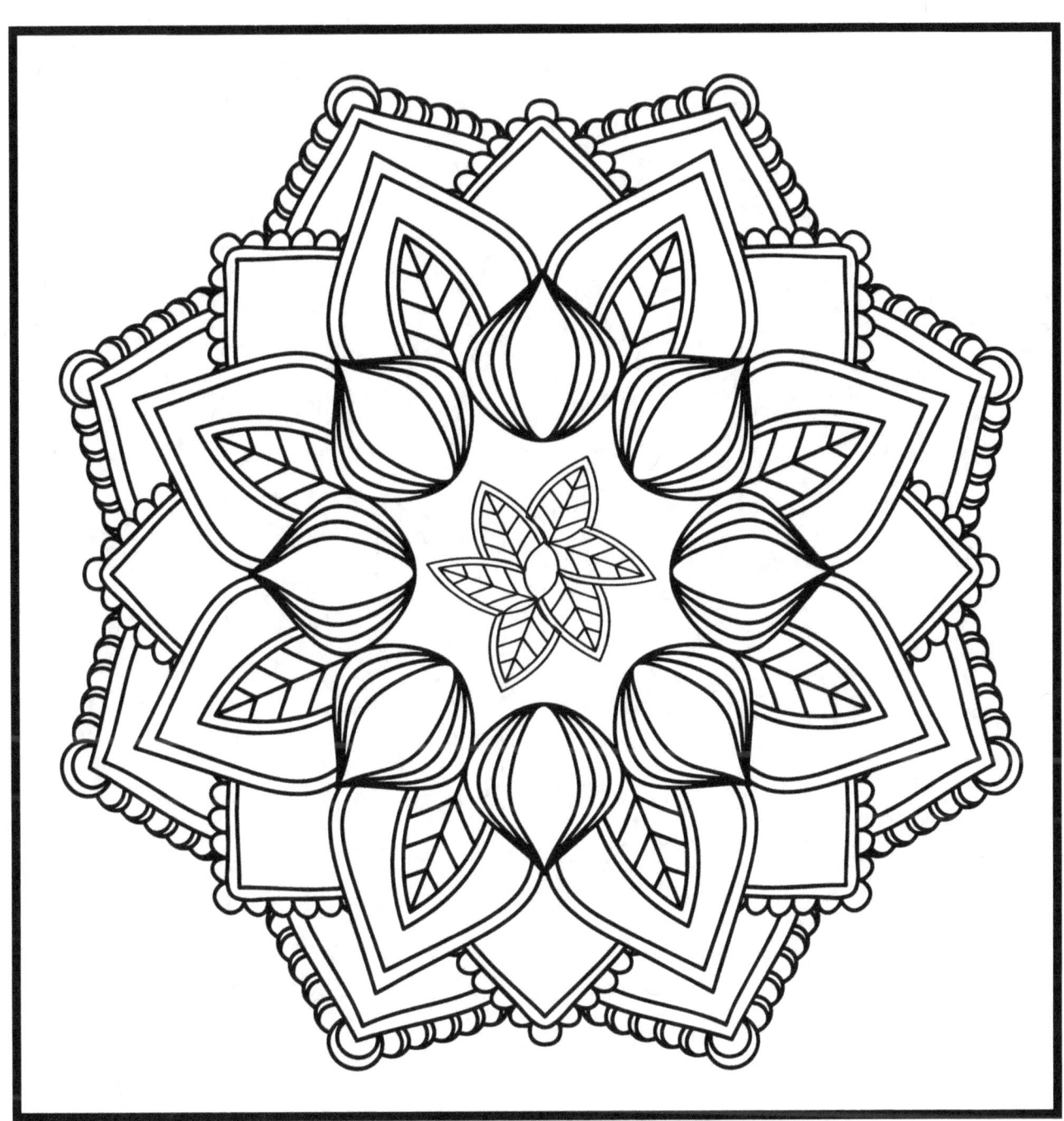

Flower Mandala

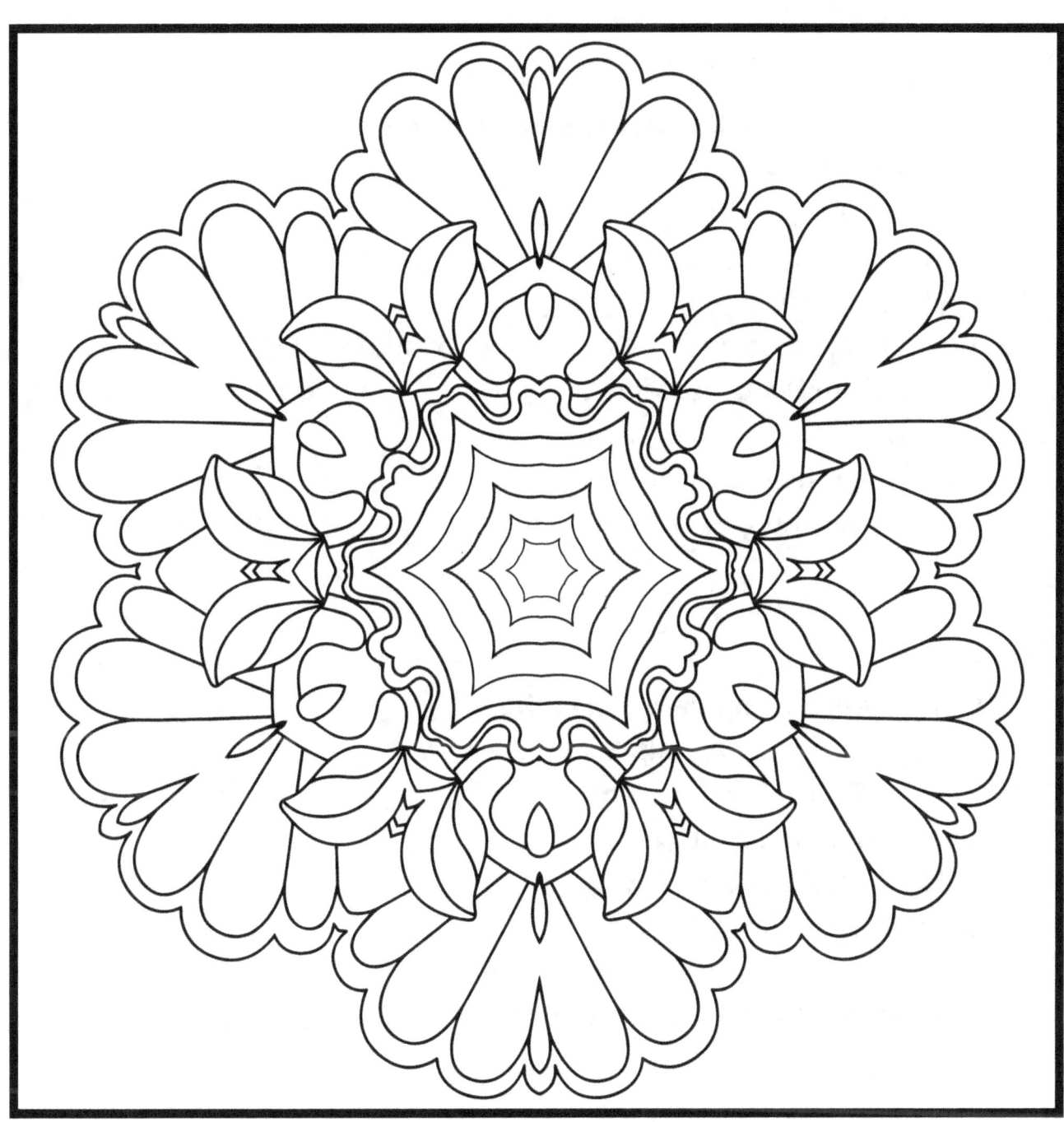

Clues for the Crossword Puzzle where you fill in a word that relates to the Activity a Winged Bug is doing on one of the pages in this book.

ACROSS

2. Derrick Dragonfly is delivering an important _____.
4. Beette Beetle is playing many _____.
5. Laci Ladybug is sitting on a _____.
6. Lizbeth Butterfly is smiling as she flies under a _____.
8. Layla is playing a _____.
12. Moki Mosquito is a _____ of an insect orchestra.
13. Cecyla Rain Beetle is doing a _____ to music floating in the air.
15. Frankie Firefly is delivering a _____.
16. Gracie Grasshopper is dancing to the _____ on a summer day.

DOWN

1. Many bugs are enjoying a beautiful _____ day.
2. Brandy Bee came to help Brianna Bee with _____ a fence.
3. Freddie Fly is sitting on a hay bale _____ a sandwich.
7. Brianna Bee is painting a _____.
9. Betsy Bumble Bee is picking _____.
10. Gaga Grasshopper is dancing in a _____ field.
11. Betsy Bumble Bee is walking in a _____ of flowers.
14. Freddie Fly is enjoying a sandwich for _____.

A Crossword Puzzle where you fill in a word that relates to the Activity a Winged Bug is doing on one of the pages in this book.

Find the Solution on page 105.

Clues for the Winged Bugs Glossary Crossword Puzzle.

ACROSS

1. Betsy is a _____.
2. Beette is a _____.
3. There are many _____ in this coloring book.
5. Gracie and Gaga are dancing _____.
8. Layrue is a _____.
9. Frankie is a _____.
10. A bug is also known as an _____.
11. There is a _____ butterfly on page 57.

DOWN

1. Lizbeth is a big smiling _____.
3. Brandy and Brianna are _____.
4. Moki is a _____.
6. Derrick is a _____.
7. Freddie is a _____.

Winged Bugs Glossary Crossword Puzzle.

Find the Solution on page 107.

Clues for the Crossword Puzzle where you answer questions with the Name of a Winged Bug.

ACROSS

4. Who met with Brandy Bee to paint a fence? _____
5. Who is Gracie Grasshopper dancing with in a grassy field? _____
6. Who is delivering a light bulb to a friend's house? _____
8. Who is walking in a field filled with flowers? _____
9. Who is helping Brianna Bee paint a fence? _____
11. Who had a conversation with Layrue Ladybug on a leafy vine? _____
12. Who is the rain beetle dancing on a very large flower? _____
13. Who is conducting the music floating over a grassy field? _____

DOWN

1. Who is the grasshopper dancing with Gaga Grasshopper? _____
2. Who is eating his lunch on a stack of hay bales? _____
3. Who met Laci Ladybug on a leafy vine? _____
7. Who is a big smiling butterfly flying under a rainbow? _____
8. Who is playing many percussion instruments? _____
10. Who is the Dragonfly looking to deliver a package? _____
11. Who is playing a guitar on a tree branch? _____

A Crossword Puzzle where you answer questions with the Name of a Winged Bug.

Find the Solution on page 109.

Tiny Flower Mandala

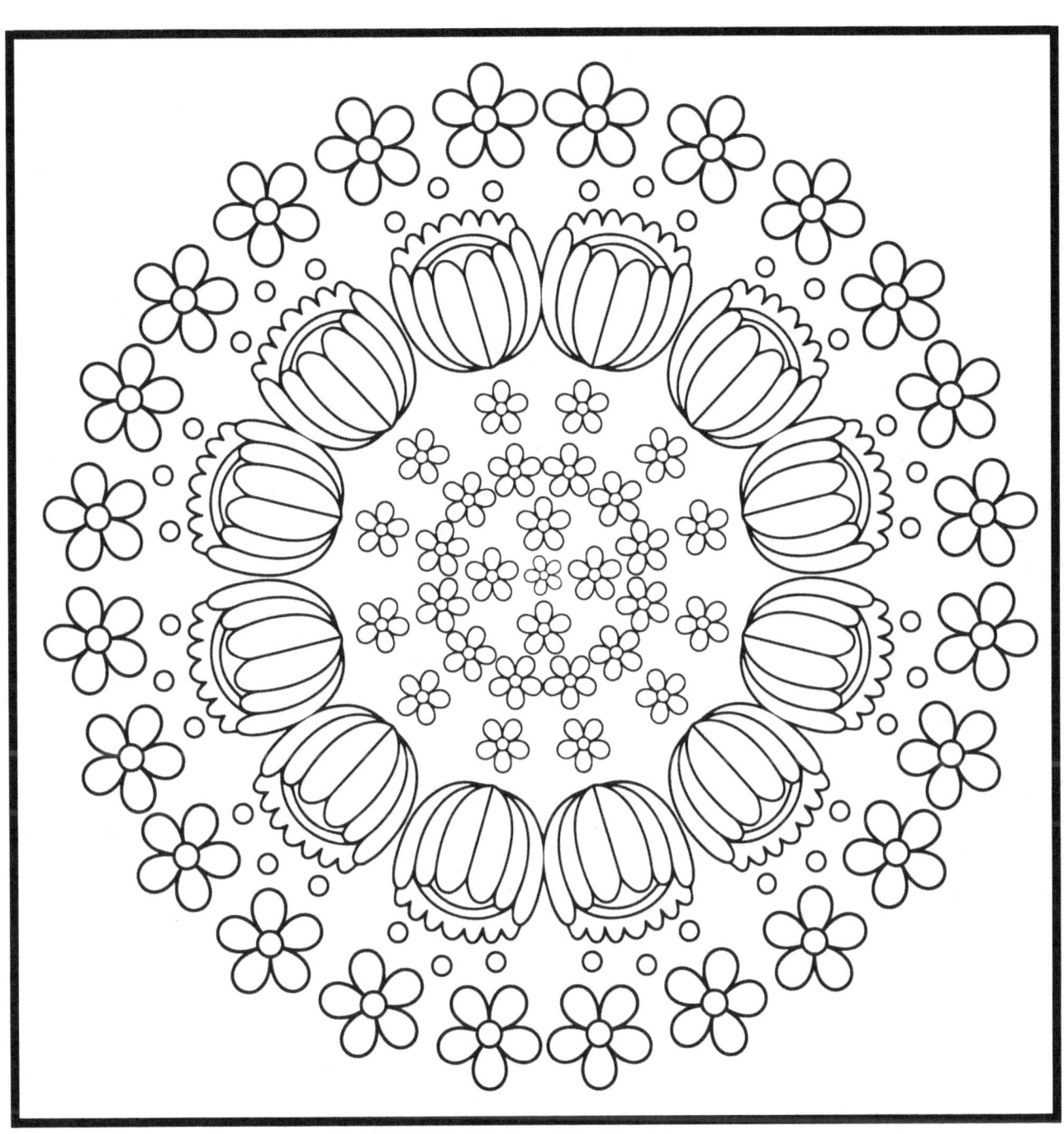

Tiny Flower Mandala

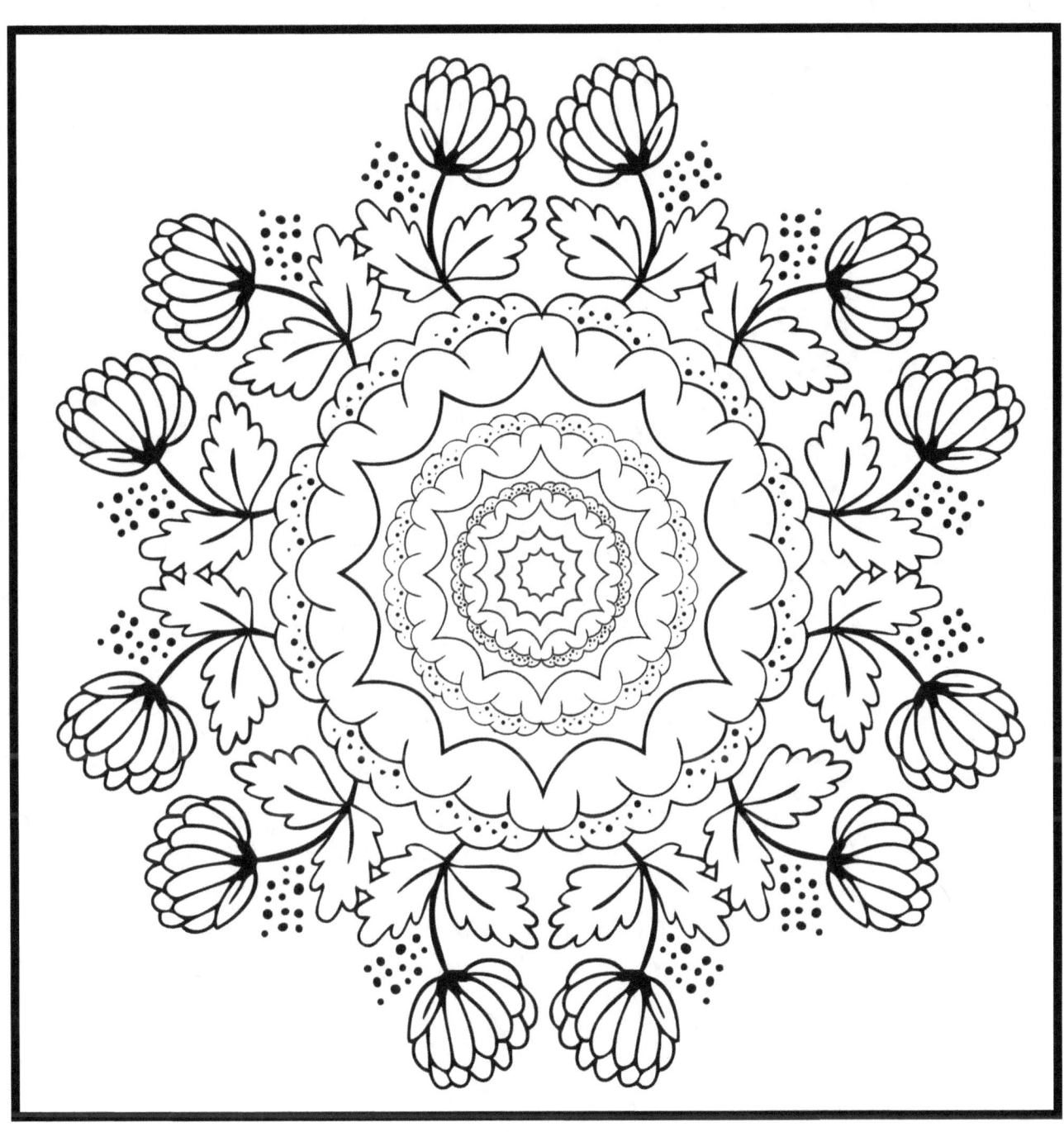

Tiny Butterfly Mandala

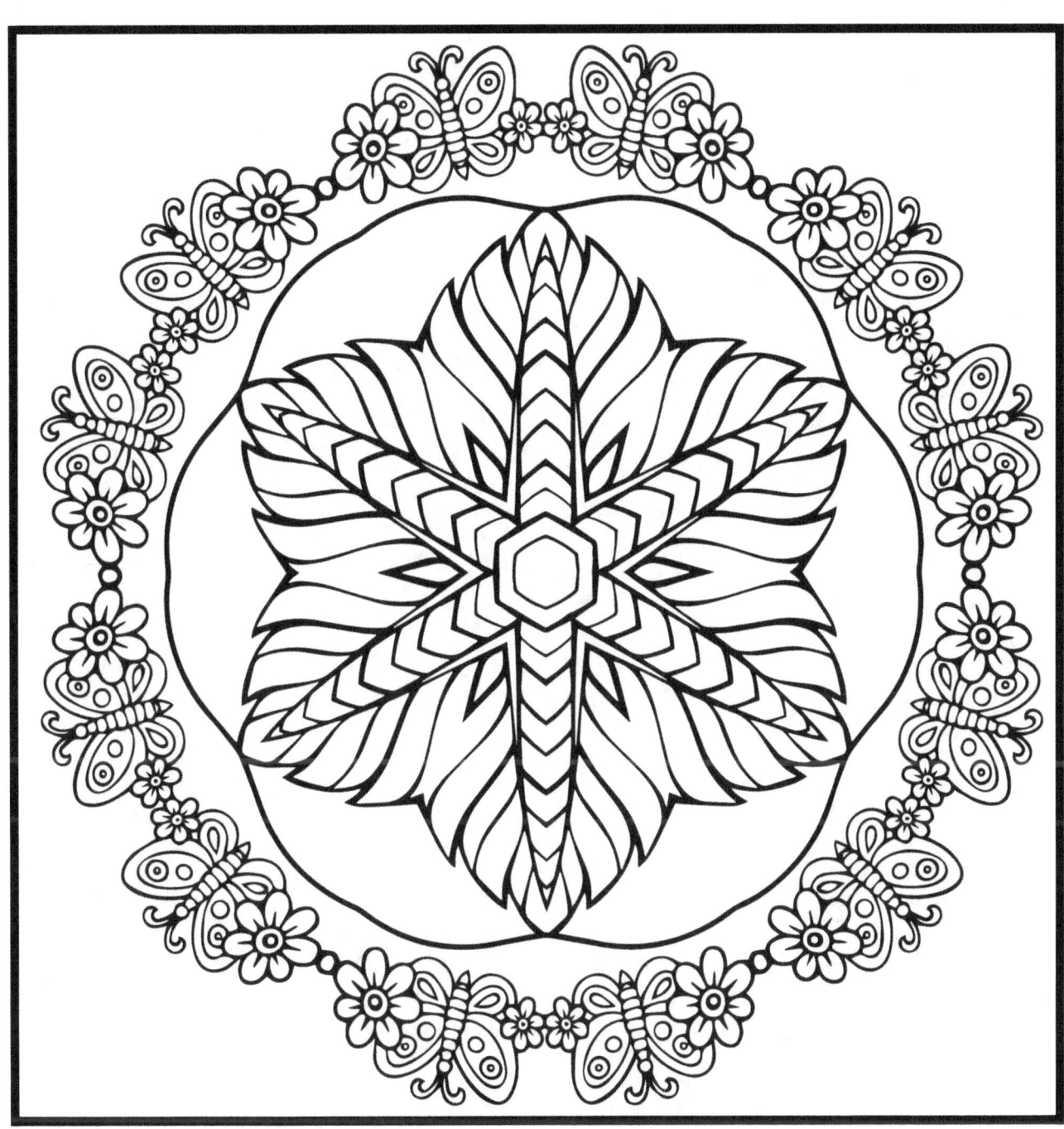

Tiny Butterfly and Flower Mandala

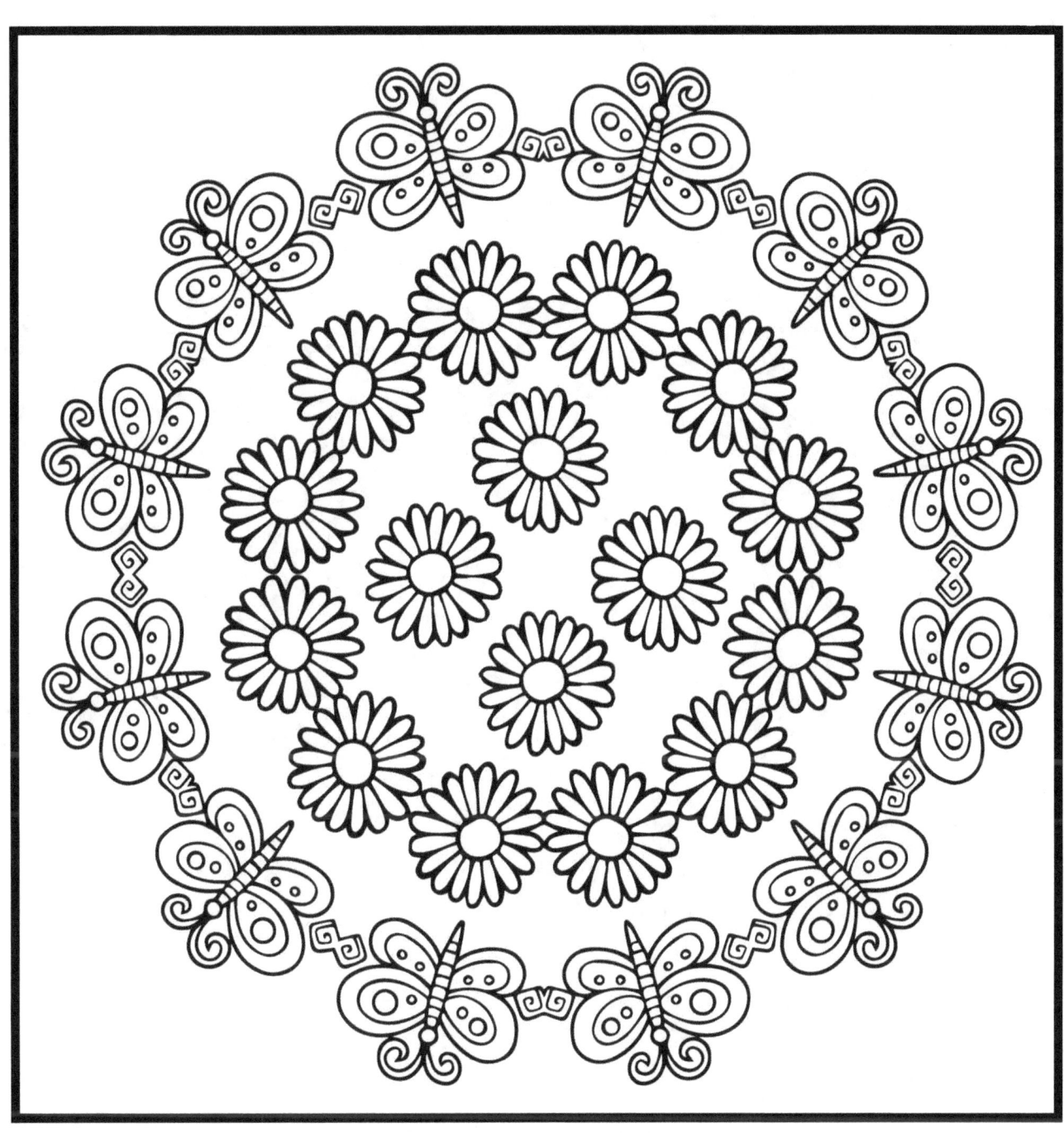

Tiny Butterfly and Flower Mandala

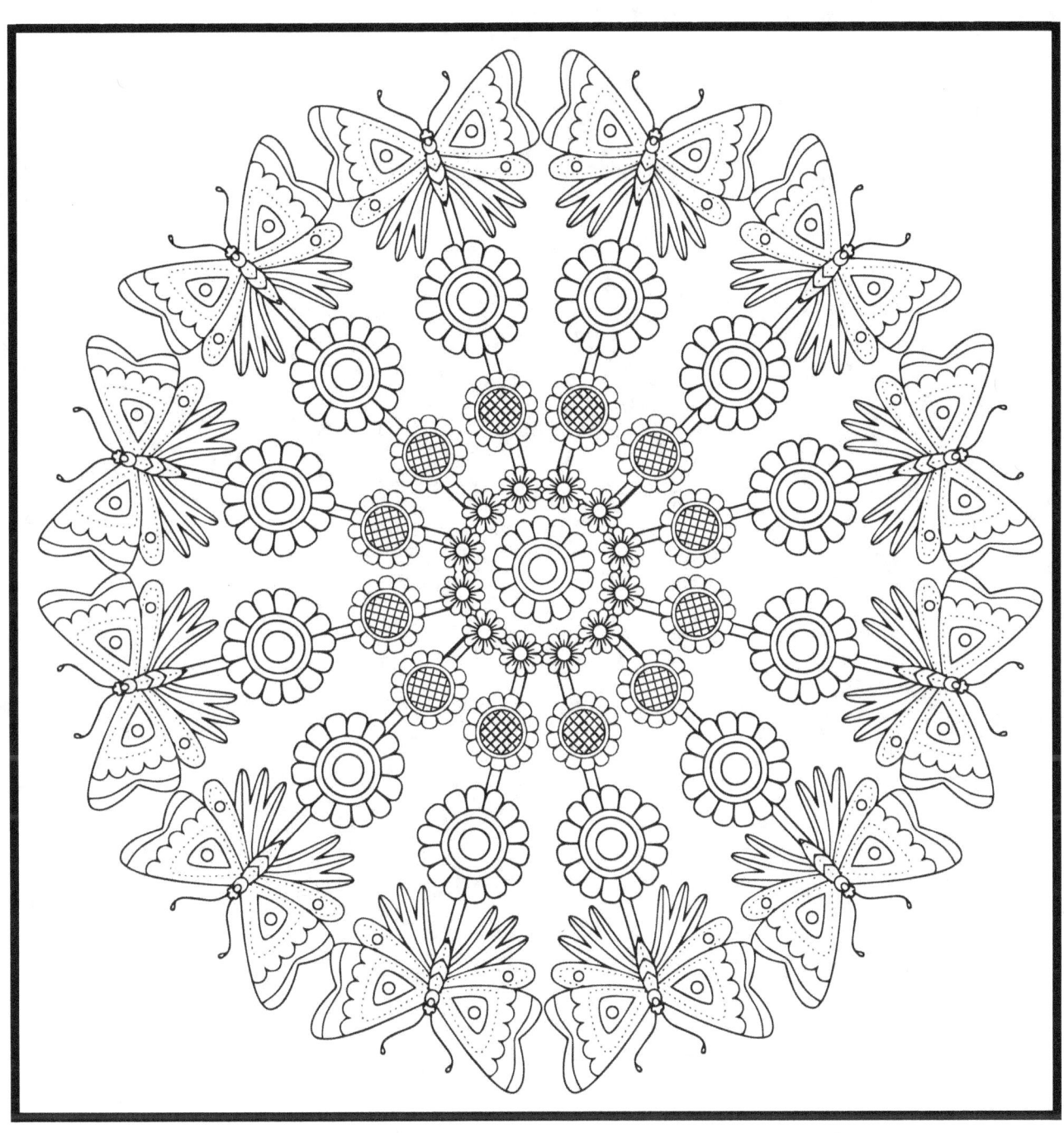

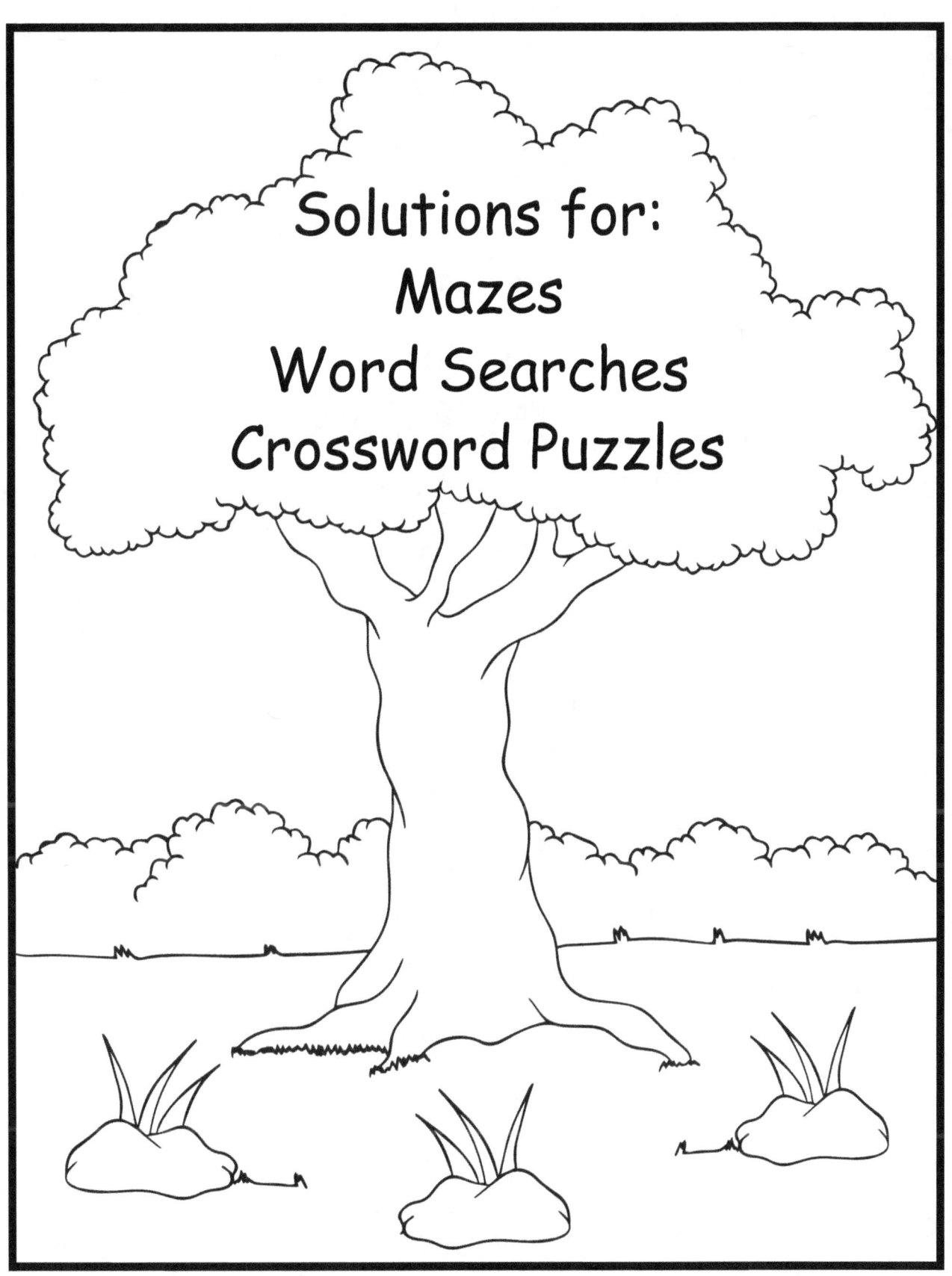

Solutions for:
Mazes
Word Searches
Crossword Puzzles

Solution for Butterfly Maze on page 29.

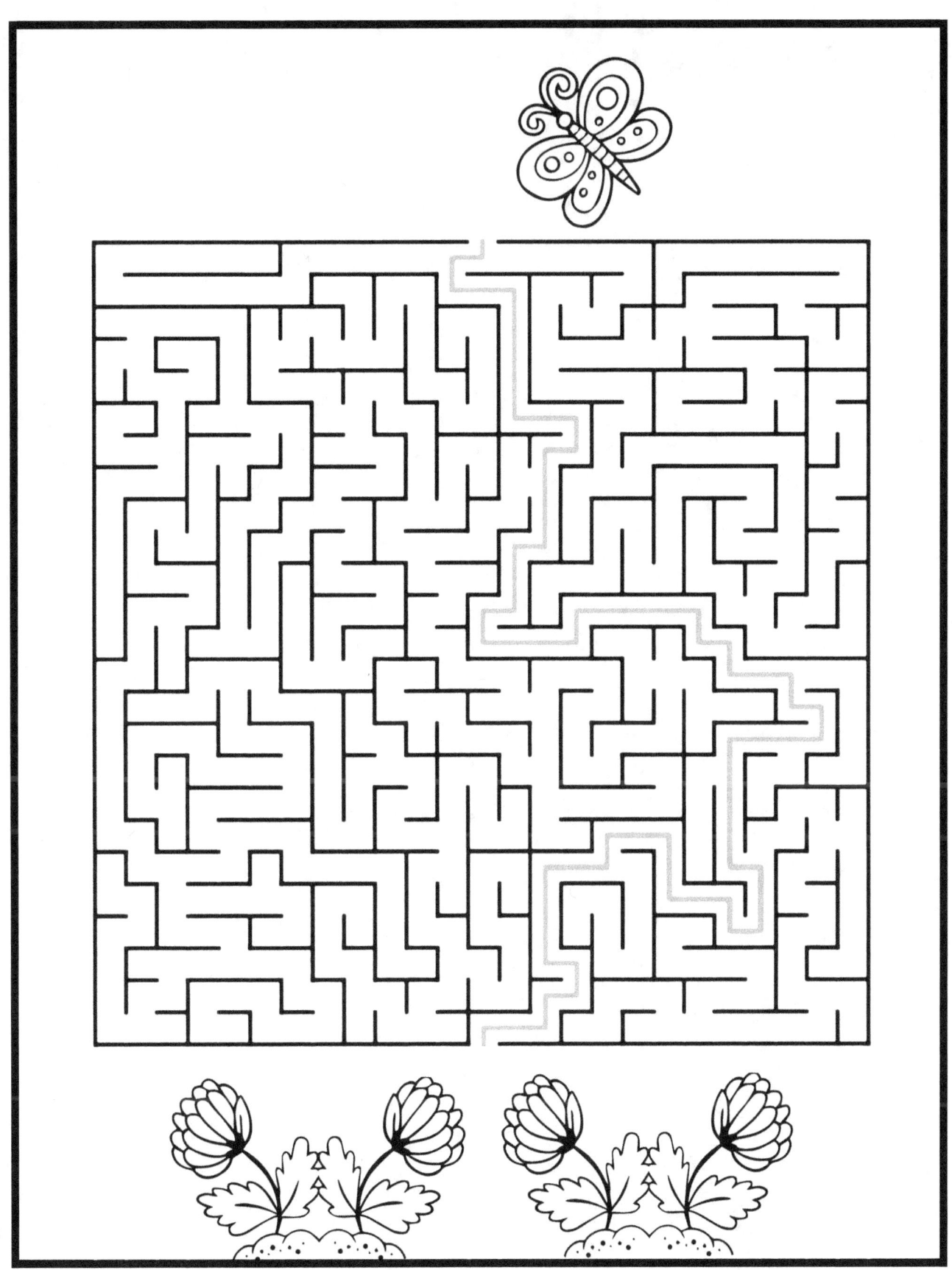

Solution for Butterfly Maze on page 31.

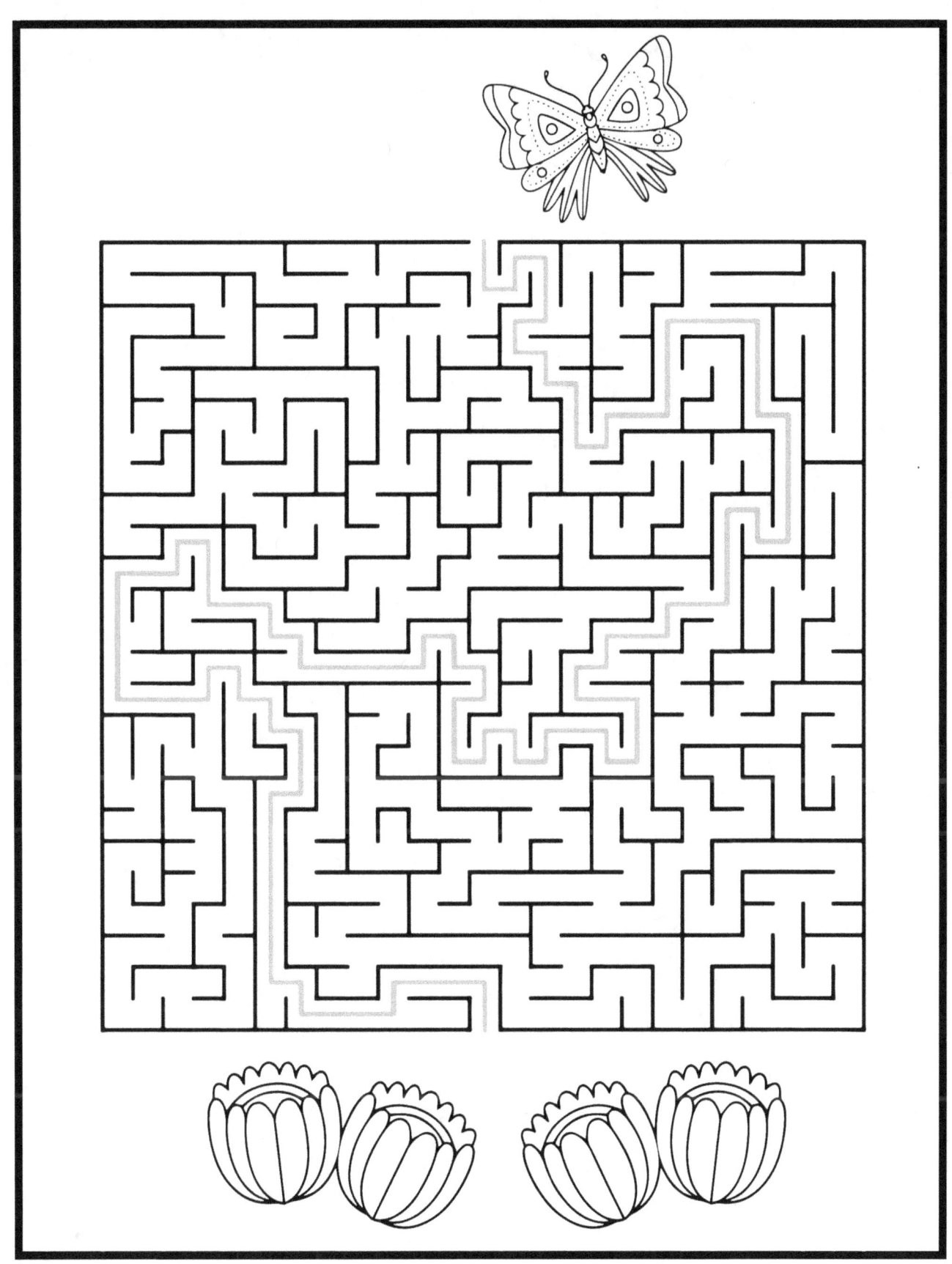

Solution for Butterfly Maze on page 33.

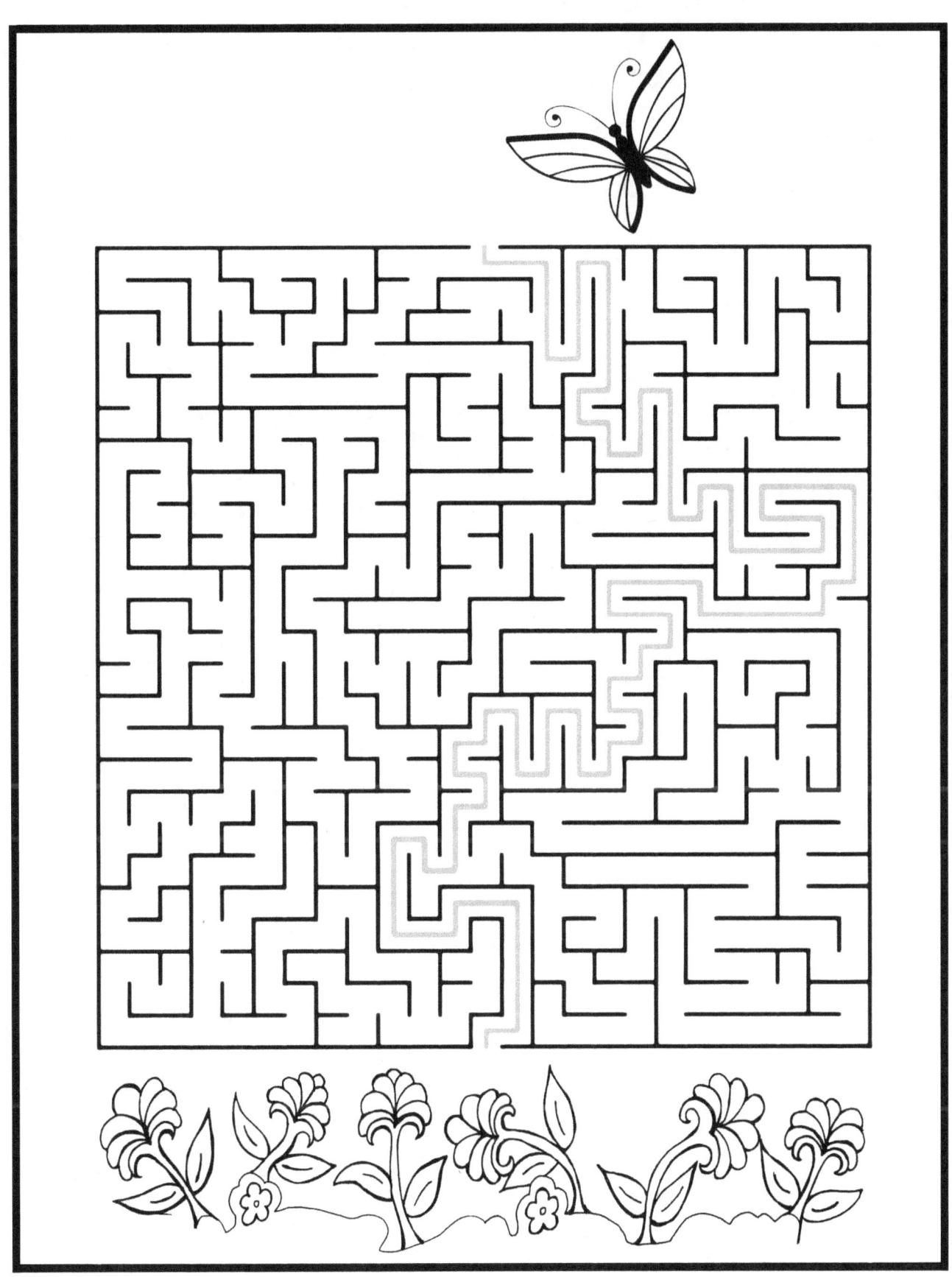

Solution for the Butterfly Maze on page 35.

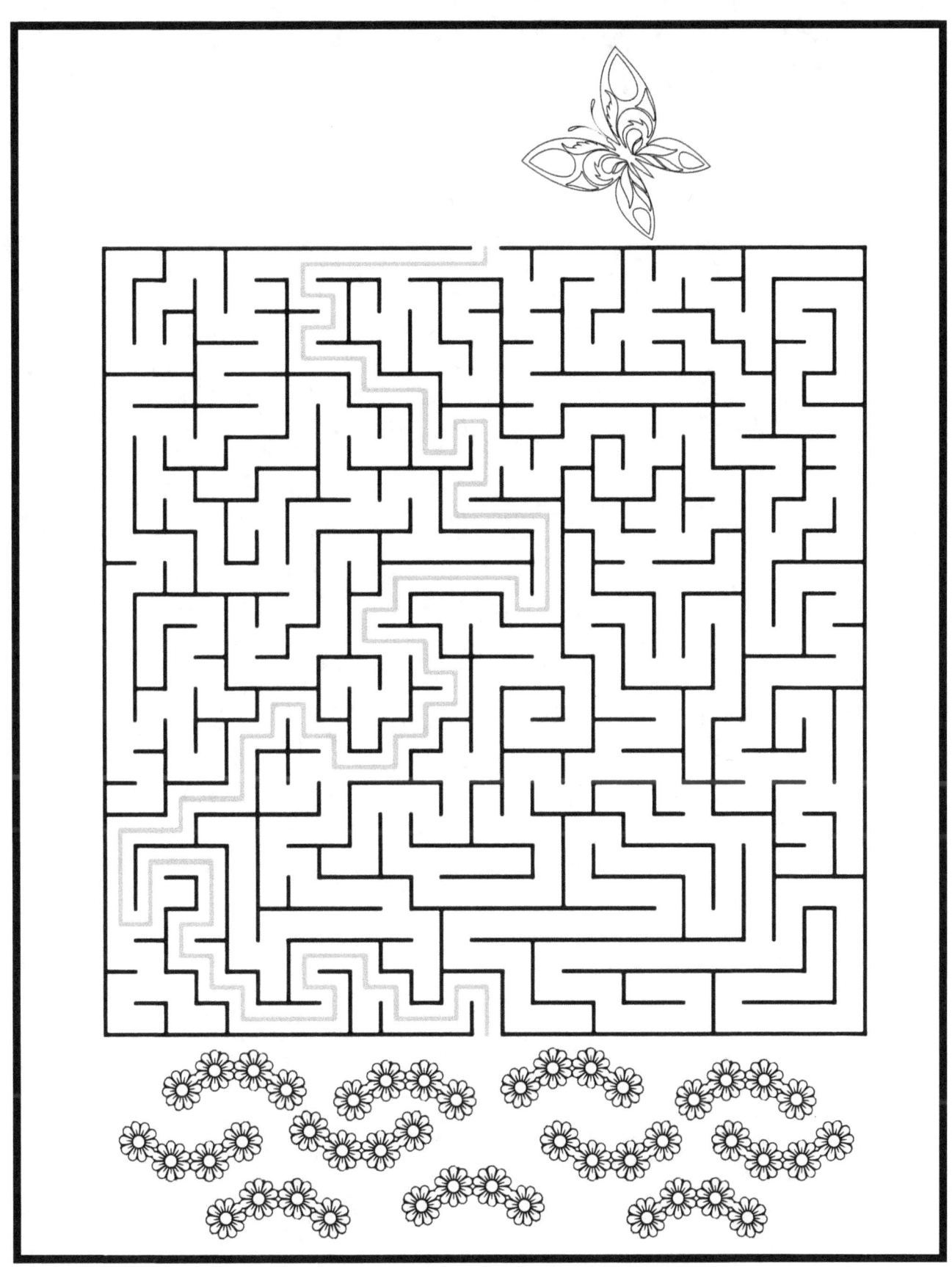

Solution for Butterfly Maze on page 37.

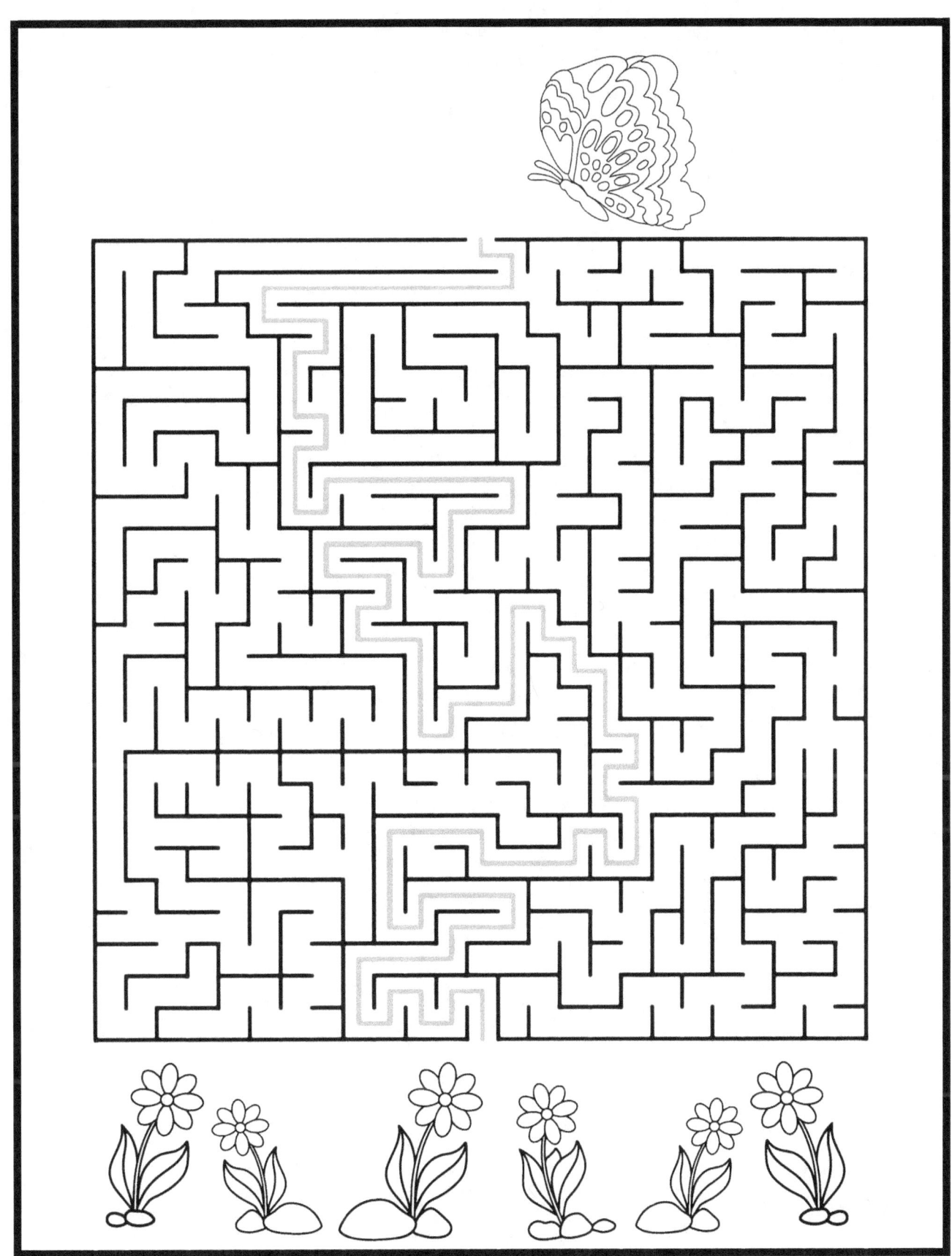

Solution for Butterfly Maze on page 39.

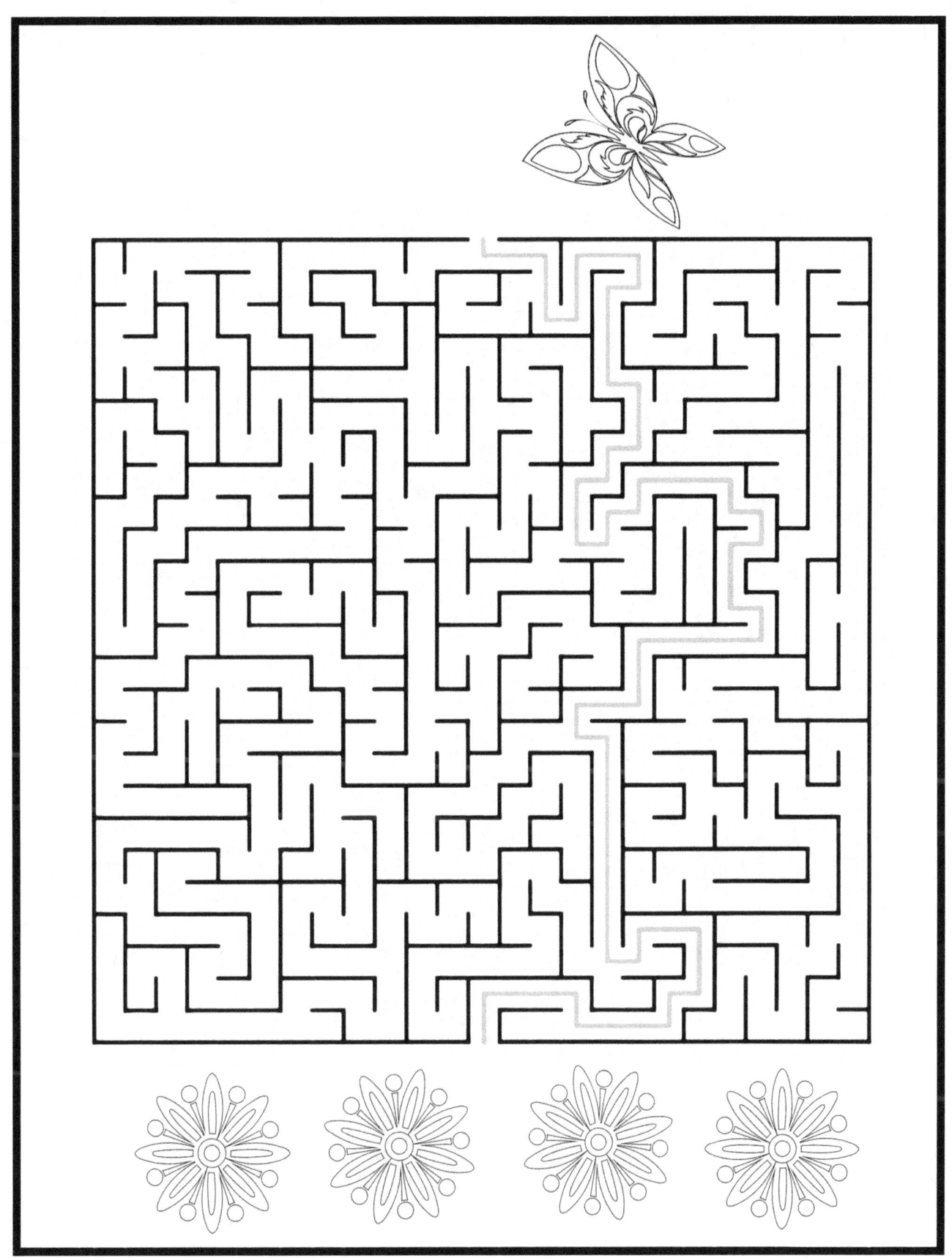

You can find a downloadable PDF of mazes
and more on Julia's ETSY shop at:
https://www.etsy.com/shop/Fantafaces

20 aMAZEing
Squirrely Fun Puzzles

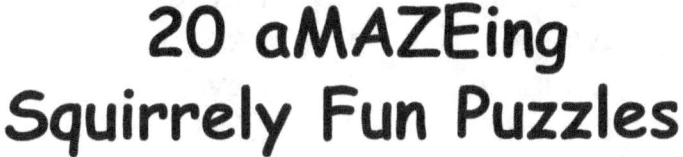

**Cute Chipmunks
and Fun-loving
Squirrels
Need Your Help
to Discover
the Trails to
Where They Store
Acorns for Winter.**

A printable book
of MAZES related to the
"Critter Activity Book"
collection created by

Julia L Wright

HieroGraphics Books

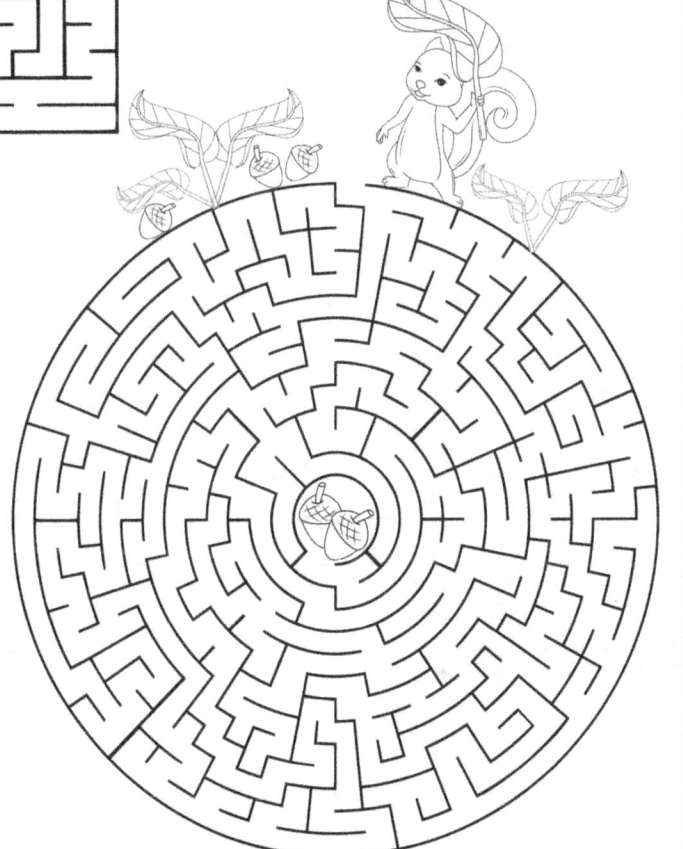

Solution for Winged Bugs Names Word Search Puzzle on Page 51.

__ Derrick   __ Betsy   __ Layla
__ Brandy   __ Laci   __ Gracie
__ Brianna   __ Layrue   __ Gaga
__ Freddie   __ Lizbeth   __ Beette
__ Frankie   __ Moki   __ Cecyla

								E	I	K	N	A	R	F	
			L	I	Z	B	E	T	H				R		
		C											E		
B	E	E	T	T	E				G				D		
			C							R			D		
			Y				A		L	A	C		I		
			L		G		L			C		E			
			A				A					I			
			G				Y						E	
		Y		Y	S	T	E	B	L					
		D				U		A						
		N		D	E	R	R	I	C	K				
		A				Y		K						
	B	R	I	A	N	N	A			O			
		B				L				M			

Solution for the Winged Bugs Glossary Word Search Puzzle on Page 53.

__ BEE   __ FLY
__ BEETLE   __ GRASSHOPPER
__ BUMBLEBEE   __ LADYBUG
__ BUTTERFLY   __ MONARCH
__ DRAGONFLY   __ MOSQUITO
__ FIREFLY   __ RAINBEETLE

										G		M		
					M	O	S	Q	U	I	T	O		
							B					N		
	F	I	R	E	F	L	Y					A		
	R			R		D		E	E	B		R		
	E			A								C		
	P			L		I				Y	H			
	P	D	R	A	G	O	N	F	L	Y	L			
	O						B			F				
	H			Y				E		R				
	S			L				E	E					
	S		F				B	E	E	T	L	E		
	A								T		L			
	R			E	E	B	E	L	B	M	U	B	E	
	G								B					

103

Winged Bugs Activities Crossword Puzzle Answers.

ACROSS

2. Derrick Dragonfly is delivering an important <u>PACKAGE</u>.
4. Beette Beetle is playing many <u>INSTRUMENTS.</u>
5. Laci Ladybug is sitting on a <u>VINE</u>.
6. Lizbeth Butterfly is smiling as she flies under a <u>RAINBOW</u>.
8. Layla is playing a <u>GUITAR</u>.
12. Moki Mosquito is a <u>CONDUCTOR</u> of an insect orchestra.
13. Cecyla Rain Beetle is doing a <u>DANCE</u> to music floating in the air.
15. Frankie Firefly is delivering a <u>LIGHT BULB</u>.
16. Gracie Grasshopper is dancing to the <u>MUSIC</u> on a summer day.

DOWN

1. Many bugs are enjoying a beautiful <u>SUMMER</u> day.
2. Brandy Bee came to help Brianna Bee with <u>PAINTING</u> a fence.
3. Freddie Fly is sitting on a hay bale <u>EATING</u> a sandwich.
7. Brianna Bee is painting a <u>FENCE</u>.
9. Betsy Bumble Bee is picking <u>FLOWERS</u>.
10. Gaga Grasshopper is dancing in a <u>GRASSY</u> field.
11. Betsy Bumble Bee is walking in a <u>FIELD</u> of flowers.
14. Freddie Fly is enjoying a sandwich for <u>LUNCH</u>.

Solution for the Winged Bugs Activities Crossword Puzzle on page 71.

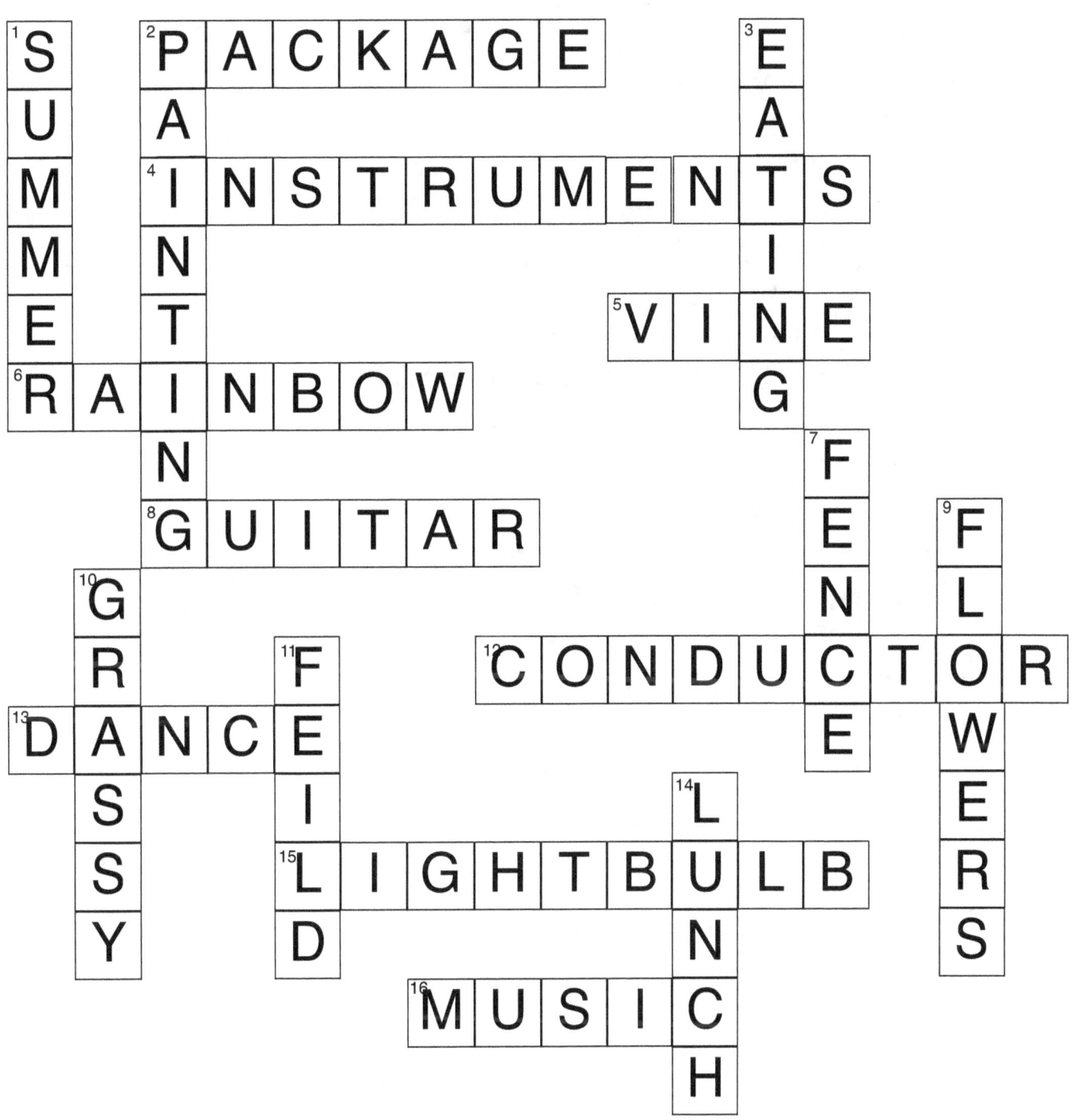

Winged Bugs Glossary Crossword Puzzle Answers.

ACROSS

1. Betsy is a <u>BUMBLEBEE</u>.
2. Beette is a <u>BEETLE</u>.
3. There are many <u>BUGS</u> in this coloring book.
5. Gracie and Gaga are dancing <u>GRASSHOPPERS</u>.
8. Layrue is a <u>LADYBUG</u>.
9. Frankie is a <u>FIREFLY</u>.
10. A bug is also known as an <u>INSECT</u>.
11. There is a <u>MONARCH</u> butterfly on page 57.

DOWN

1. Lizbeth is a big smiling <u>BUTTERFLY</u>.
3. Brandy and Brianna are <u>BEES</u>.
4. Moki is a <u>MOSQUITO</u>.
6. Derrick is a <u>DRAGONFLY</u>.
7. Freddie is a <u>FLY</u>.

Solution for the Winged Bugs Glossary
Crossword Puzzle on page 73.

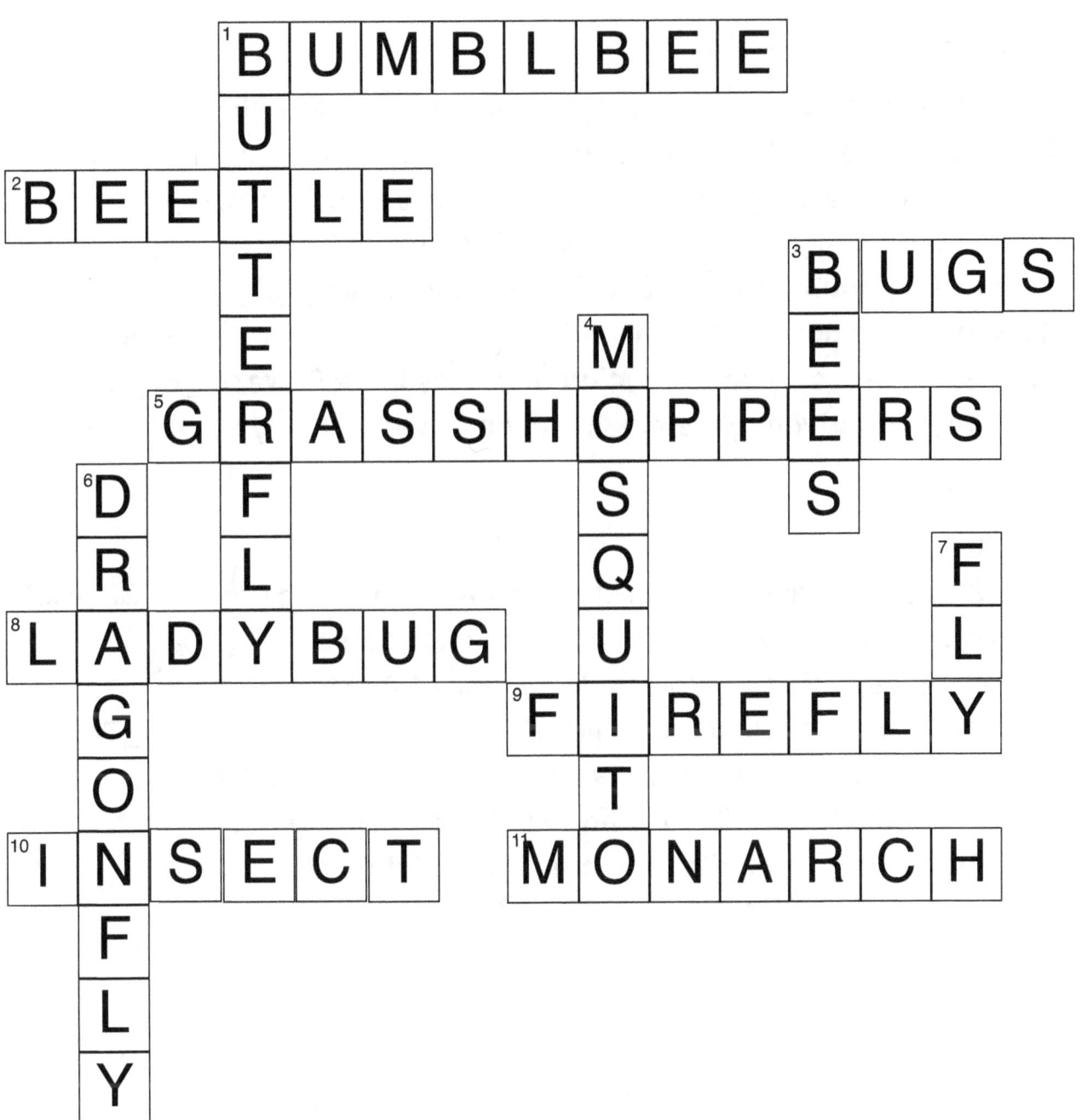

Winged Bugs Names Crossword Puzzle Answers.

ACROSS

4. Who met with Brandy Bee to paint a fence? <u>BRIANNA</u>
5. Who is Gracie Grasshopper dancing with in a grassy field? <u>GAGA</u>
6. Who is delivering a light bulb to a friend's house? <u>FRANKIE</u>
8. Who is waling in a field filled with flowers? <u>BETSY</u>
9. Who is helping Brianna Bee paint a fence? <u>BRANDY</u>
11. Who had a conversation with Layrue Ladybug on a leafy vine? <u>LACI</u>
12. Who is the rain beetle dancing on a very large flower? <u>CECYLA</u>
13. Who is conducting the music floating over a grassy field? <u>MOKI</u>

DOWN

1. Who is the grasshopper dancing with Gaga Grasshopper? <u>GRACIE</u>
2. Who is eating his lunch on a stack of hay bales? <u>FREDDIE</u>
3. Who met Laci Ladybug on a leafy vine? <u>LAYRUE</u>
7. Who is a big smiling butterfly flying under a rainbow? <u>LIZBETH</u>
8. Who is playing many percussion instruments? <u>BEETTE</u>
10. Who is the Dragonfly looking to deliver a package? <u>DERRICK</u>
11. Who is playing a guitar on a tree branch? <u>LAYLA</u>

Solution for the Winged Bugs Names Crossword Puzzle on page 75.

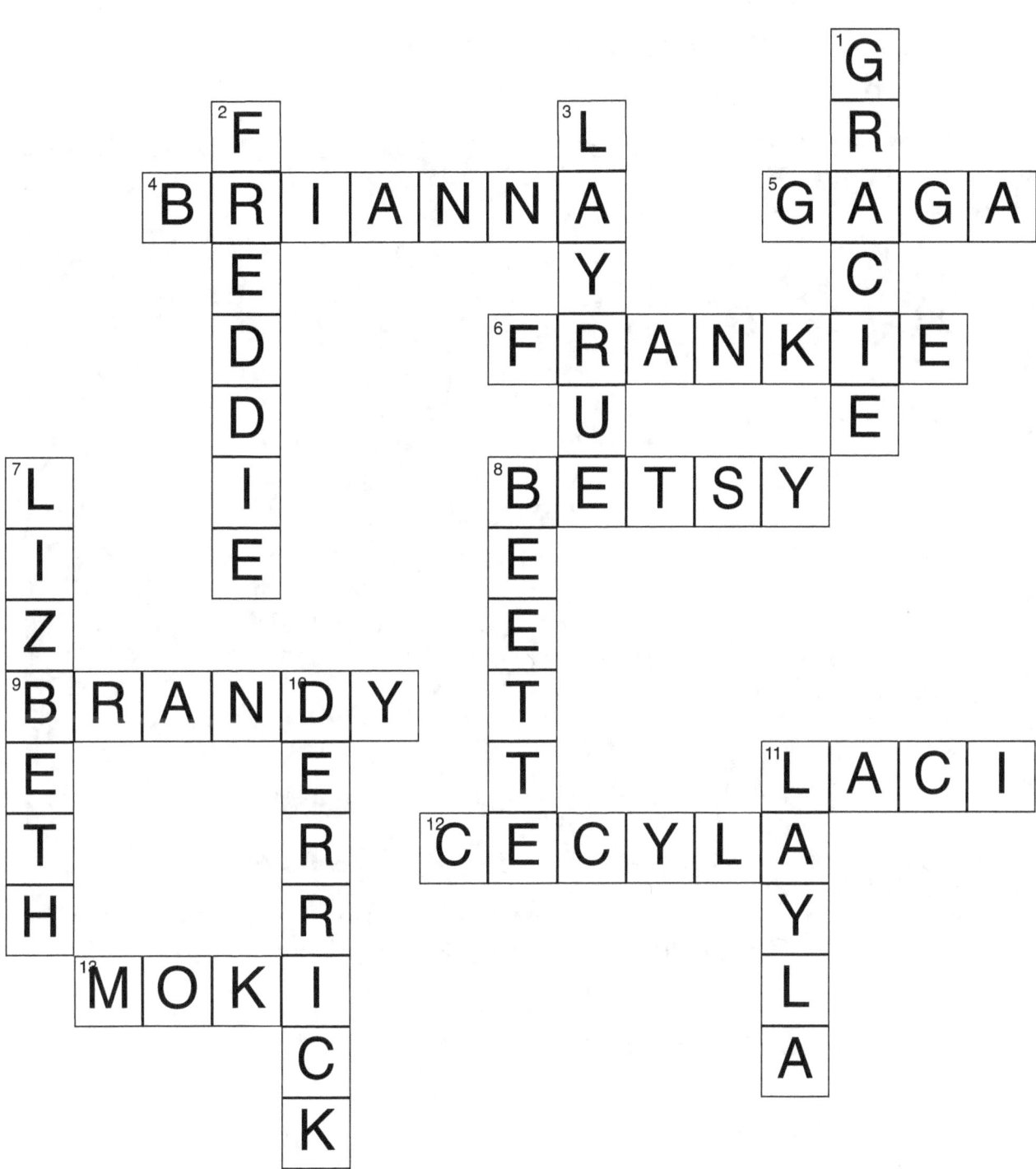

If you love bugs and butterflies, chances are you also enjoy watching squirrels at play. In Violet Burbach's and Julia L. Wright's colorfully illustrated book, "Discover The World Of Squirrels", children can learn interesting facts about these fascinating creatures that live in forests around the world.

This book includes a glossary of new words kids will be introduced to when reading the book.

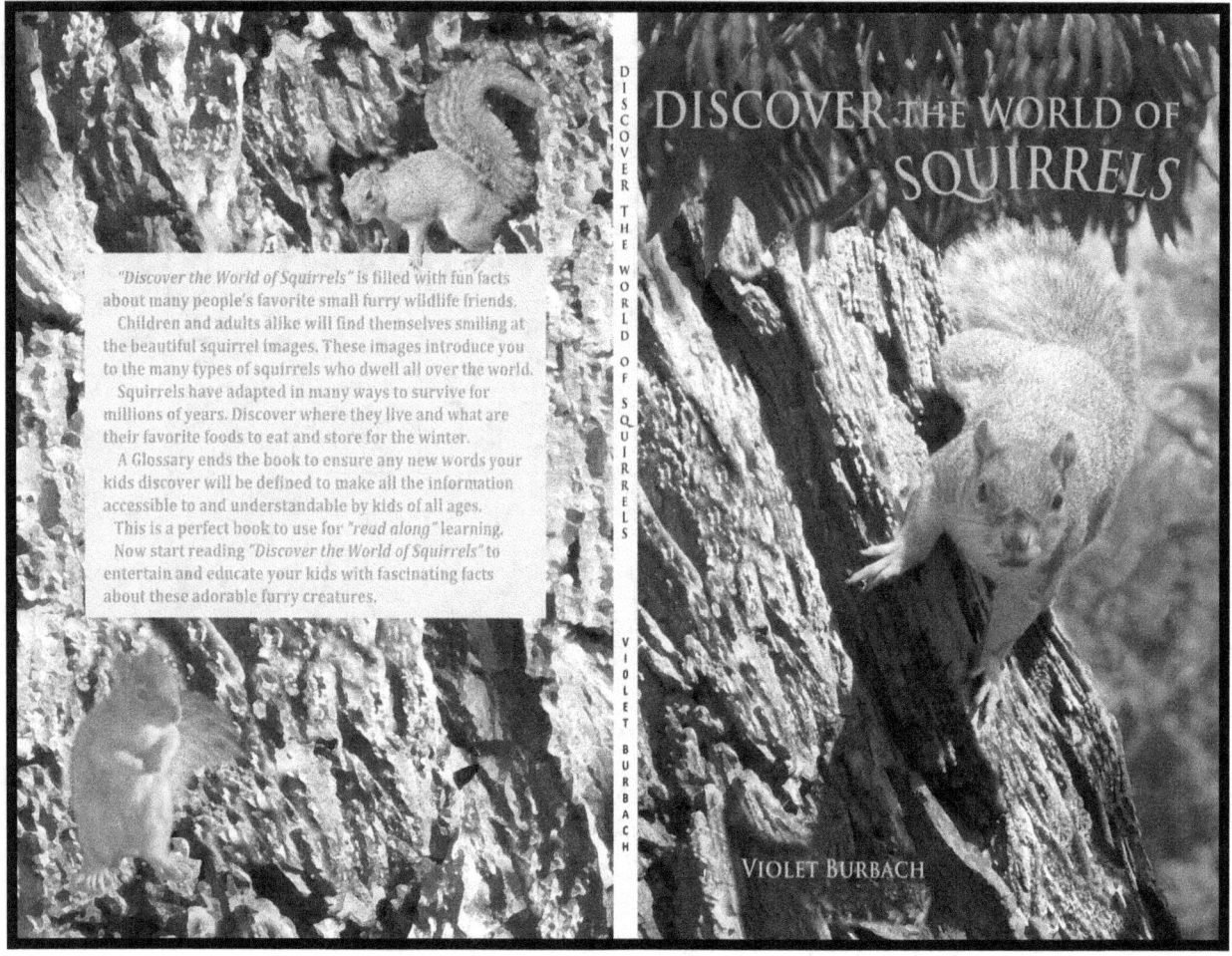

You can find this educational and fun book about squirrels on Amazon at:
https://www.amazon.com/dp/1512255335/

And if you want to learn more about chipmunks and other ground squirrels check out "Discover The World Of Ground Squirrels" at: https://www.amazon.com/dp/0996581634.

Rockey is inviting you to come explore the "Squirrel Coloring And Activity Book" from HieroGraphics Books.

www.amazon.com/dp/0996581669/

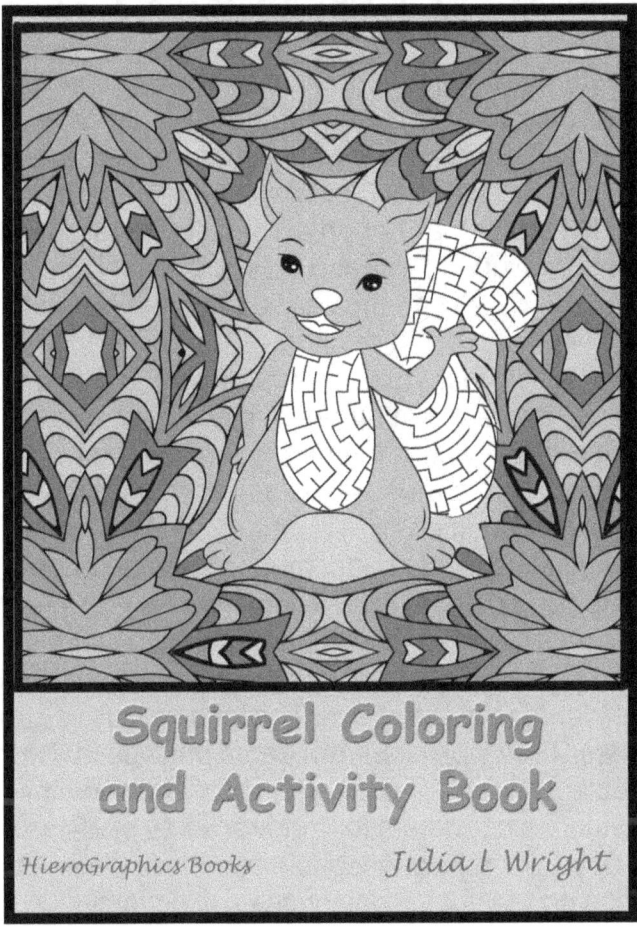

Princess Acorna would like to invite you to come explore the "Chipmunk Coloring And Activity Book" from HieroGraphics Books.

www.amazon.com/dp/0996581650/

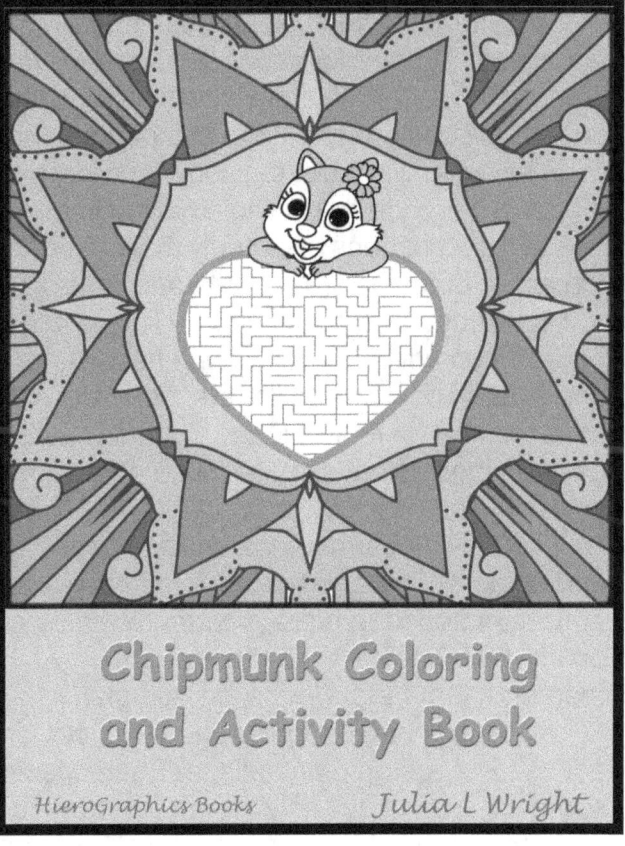

You will find these, and other coloring and activity books created by Julia L. Wright on Amazon.com.

Click on my author name to find more coloring and activities books filled with cute critters and mandalas for hours of fun.

Butterfly Facts

Butterflies can be found worldwide except Antarctica, totalling some 18,500 speciesthat have been found distributed across the combined Oriental and Australian/Oceania regions. These winged insects are members of the lepidopteran superfamily Papilionoidea. They are characterised by large, often brightly coloured wings that often fold together when at rest, and a conspicuous, fluttering, rather bumpy flight.

The oldest butterfly fossils have been dated to the Paleocene age, about 56 million years ago. Molecular evidence suggests that they likely originated during the Cretaceous period of the planet, but only significantly diversified during the Cenozoic. The oldest known American butterfly is the Late Eocene Prodryas Persephone that was discovered in the Florissant Fossil Beds, in Colorado and is approximately 34 million years old.

Butterflies evolved from moths, so while the butterflies are monophyletic (forming a single clade), the moths are not. Nearly all butterflies can only be seen during the day. They have relatively bright colours, and hold their wings vertically above their bodies when at rest. The colour of butterfly wings is derived from tiny structures called scales, each of which have their own pigments. Whereas the majority of moths, which fly by night, are often cryptically coloured to be well camouflages, and either hold their wings flat (touching the surface on which the moth is standing) or fold them closely over their bodies. Some day-flying moths, such as the hummingbird hawk-moth, are exceptions to these rules.

Butterflies in their adult stage can live from a week to nearly a year depending on the species. Many butterflies, such as the painted lady, monarch, and several others migrate over long distances. These migrations take place over a number of generations and no single individual completes the whole trip. Butterflies navigate using a time-compensated sun compass. They can see polarised light and therefore orient even in cloudy conditions.

Similar to all insects, the body is divided into three sections: the head, thorax, and abdomen. The thorax of the butterfly is devoted to locomotion and is composed of three segments, each with a pair of legs. In most families of butterfly the antennae are clubbed, unlike those of moths which may be threadlike or feathery. The abdomen consists of ten segments and contains the gut and genital organs.

Adult butterflies consume only liquids, ingested through the proboscis. The long proboscis can be coiled when not in use for sipping nectar from flowers. They sip water from damp patches for hydration and feed on nectar from flowers, from which they obtain sugars for energy, and sodium and other minerals vital for reproduction. Butterflies are important as pollinators for many species of plants. In general, they do not carry as much pollen load as bees, but they are capable of moving pollen over greater distances. Flower constancy has been observed for at least one species of butterfly.

Butterflies use their antennae to sense the air for wind and scents and come in various shapes and colours. The antennae are richly covered with sensory organs known as sensillae. A butterfly's sense of taste is coordinated by chemoreceptors on the tarsi, or feet, which work only on contact. They are used to determine whether an egg-laying insect's offspring will be able to feed on a leaf before eggs are laid on it.

Butterflies have a four-stage life cycle, and they undergo a complete metamorphosis. Winged adults lay eggs on plant foliage. Each species of butterfly has its own host plant range and while some species of butterfly are restricted to just one species of plant, others use a range of plant species, often including members of a common family. When the caterpillars emerge, they will feed on those leaves. Although most caterpillars are herbivorous, a few species are predators.

Caterpillars

Caterpillars have short antennae and several simple eyes. The mouthparts are adapted for chewing with powerful mandibles and a pair of maxillae, each with a segmented palp. When a Caterpillar is fully grown, it stops feeding, and begins "wandering" in the quest for a suitable pupation site, often the underside of a leaf or other concealed location to spin a button of silk.

The naked pupa, often known as a chrysalis, usually hangs head down from the cremaster, a spiny pad at the posterior end. Most of the tissues and cells of the larva are broken down inside the pupa, as the constituent material is rebuilt into the imago. The structure of the transforming insect is visible from the exterior, with the wings folded flat on the ventral surface and the two halves of the proboscis, with the antennae and the legs between them.

When metamorphosis is complete, the pupal skin splits, the adult insect climbs out. After it emerges from its pupal stage, a butterfly cannot fly until the wings are unfolded. A newly emerged butterfly needs to spend some time inflating its wings with hemolymph and letting them dry.

Declining butterfly populations have been noticed in many areas of the world, and this phenomenon is consistent with the rapidly decreasing insect populations around the world. Queen Alexandra's birdwing, found in Papua New Guinea, is the largest butterfly in the world. The species is endangered, and is one of only three insects that are listed in a way that makes international trade of them illegal. In the Western United States, this collapse in the number of most species of butterflies has been determined to be driven by global climate change, specifically, by warmer autumns. Butterfly populations in the United States declined by 22% between 2000 and 2020, mainly because of habitat loss, pesticides and climate change.

Beautiful Butterflies

Butterflies are a popular motif in every culture around the world in the visual and literary arts. Many states in the USA have chosen an official state butterfly. Many peoplebelieve that butterflies are one of the most appealing and beautiful creatures in nature.

Butterflies have appeared in art from 3500 years ago in ancient Egypt. In hunting scenes, butterflies were sometimes included in a way that suggested life, freedom, and the strength to escape capture. They also were suggestive of regeneration or rebirth and protection. Certain butterflies, such as the tiger butterfly, may have been associated with solar deities, particularly Ra. The tiger butterfly also would have a particular resemblance to the ankh, due to its black body and wingtips, that was likely noted by the Ancient Egyptians. Butterflies may also have been understood as one of the deceased's guides in the afterlife.

In the ancient Mesoamerican city of Teotihuacan in Mexico, the brilliantly coloured image of the butterfly was carved into many temples, buildings, jewellery, and emblazoned on incense burners. The butterfly was sometimes depicted with the maw of a jaguar, and some species were considered to be the reincarnations of the souls of dead warriors. The close association of butterflies with fire and warfare persisted into the Aztec civilisation; evidence of similar jaguar-butterfly images has been found among the Zapotec and Maya civilisations.

In some cultures, butterflies are seen as a sybol of for the soul. The ancient Greek word for "butterfly" is ψυχή (psȳchē), which primarily means "soul" or "mind". In popular Burmese culture, the butterfly is symbolic of the soul or consciousness of a person. The Burmese believe that the "butterfly soul" becomes a wandering spirit in search of a new coporeality medium during the transitory period after death. In some cultures, butterflies symbolise rebirth. Butterflies are widely used in objects of art and jewellery: mounted in frames, embedded in resin, displayed in bottles, laminated in paper, and used in some mixed media artworks and furnishings.

Butterflies and caterpillars are often found in literature and illustrations of those books. In 1865, Sir John Tenniel drew an illustration of Alice meeting a caterpillar for Lewis Carroll's Alice in Wonderland. The caterpillar is seated on a toadstool and is smoking a hookah. A butterfly appeared in one of Rudyard Kipling's Just So Stories, "The Butterfly that Stamped".

Now is the Time For You to Color or Write a Story or Draw a Butterfly

Think about how no snowflakes are alike, and set in motion your creativity by coloring each one in this book however you choose. Each time you color one of the butterflies in this book, you create a unique version of this fanciful creature that will never be the same as another one. What story might you write about a butterfly? Or draw and color to illustrate an idea in that story? Have Fun!

Aspiring artists can use this page to create an image for your story.

Give your story a title using the Winged Bug's name and what he or she is doing. Then have fun telling a story about what this bug will do next, starting with the scene on the page you are writing this story about.

TITLE: _____

_____

_____

_____

_____

_____

_____

_____

_____

_____

_____

_____

_____

_____

_____

_____

_____

_____

Aspiring artists can use this page to create an image for your story.

Give your story a title using the Winged Bug's name and what he or she is doing. Then have fun telling a story about what this bug will do next, starting with the scene on the page you are writing this story about.

TITLE: _____

_____

_____

_____

_____

_____

_____

_____

_____

_____

_____

_____

_____

_____

Aspiring artists can use this page to create an image for your story.

Give your story a title using the Winged Bug's name and what he or she is doing. Then have fun telling a story about what this bug will do next, starting with the scene on the page you are writing this story about.

TITLE: _____

_____

_____

_____

_____

_____

_____

_____

_____

_____

_____

_____

_____

_____

Aspiring artists can use this page to create an image for your story.

Give your story a title using the Winged Bug's name and what he or she is doing. Then have fun telling a story about what this bug will do next, starting with the scene on the page you are writing this story about.

TITLE: _____

_____

_____

_____

_____

_____

_____

_____

_____

_____

_____

_____

_____

_____

www.ingramcontent.com/pod-product-compliance
Lightning Source LLC
Chambersburg PA
CBHW080416290526
45791CB00008BA/2300